Cat Tales

David R. Torrence

Frontier Dreamer Publications

frontierdreamer@wmconnect.com

Published by Frontier Dreamer Publications
2070 Bruceville Road
Meherrin, VA 23954
434/736-8375

ISBN: 978-0-9774220-4-3

Library of Congress Control Number: 2010921571

Printed in the United States of America
Farmville, Virginia

INTRODUCTION

This book is a random collection of my remembrances of some experiences I had in my lifetime with Felix Domesticus; the not so common pussycat. In that they have all gone on or forgotten me, I have not forgotten them. I felt compelled to write about them before they slipped forever from my mind and from the world. Cats obviously have no literary tradition of their own to capture their exploits and notable characters.

The world is comprised of cat people, cat lovers, cat haters, and those in between. Please note that I make the distinction between cat people and cat lovers. Cat people are those people who find cats to be the culturally and intellectually superior beings. They, of course, would take issue with even this objective observation. Cat people have difficulty defining the boundaries between being a human and being a cat. I fall somewhere between a cat lover and a cat owner. I just find them fascinating.

So, in order to appeal to readers comprising cat people, cat lovers, cat owners, and even cat haters, dog people and psychology majors, I have written these stories as objectively as possible. They are all true. Some written shortly after their observation, others from memories burned into my brain. So please excuse me if you find me shifting the tense of these stories from the present to the past tense. *For instance, Bob, my cat that features prominently in a couple of stories has now passed on.*

Like most young boys growing up in the inner-city, cats, like rats and starlings, were just there. *Growing up in the city was to grow up with dogs, not cats.* To borrow a segment from my dog story recollections, I must admit to having been a cat hater for a time. *Here is what I admitted to in one of my dog stories:*

"In that the inner-city neighborhood existed in such a restricted physical space and that the myriad of children routinely passed in and out of neighboring houses, the local dogs must have perceived the entire neighborhood as the extended pack. All the dogs in the neighborhood knew every other dog and seemed to live amicably with one another.

Cats were another story. In that cats usually are not pack animals, they were never recognized as belonging. Indeed, Nosey, a neighborhood dog, hated cats. She had a reputation of being a cat killer. If a cat was caught in the open in the public domain, it was doomed. Nosey, who never moved beyond a snail's pace in the normal course of a day, would go into frenzy when she saw a cat. Now inner-city neighborhoods house two types of people. The majority were young families with scads of children. The minority was elderly women whose families were reared and husbands deceased. In that they really had nothing in common with their younger and noisier neighbors, they didn't integrate to a great degree. These constituted the cat owners in the neighborhood. We kids, with our dogs and balls, made their life a living hell, much to my shame as I now approach their age."

But over the years, I met some cats that gave every impression of being quite like me: fellow mortal beings in this vale of tears. My first cat came with my first wife. Indeed, had my wife had the personality of her cat, there may well have never been the need to call her "my first." By realizing that they are brother and sister saints and sinners like us "paragon of animals", I came to admire and even love cats.

While I love them, I can't claim to be a "cat person" using the definition I've spelled out earlier in my writing. My aunt and cousin were real cat people. When I visited their house, it became obvious that not only did I occupy an inferior status in their household relative to their cats, as there were many; but that they too occupied an inferior status. They had willingly become the slaves of their cats. My congratulations to their cats, the superior beings!

Table of Contents

.

About the author:

Dave Torrence, after many years in public and collegiate education, retired to a rural life in southern Virginia. Since then, he has devoted much of his time to his lifelong love of writing.

His first novel: **A Gentleman on the Frontier** was published in 2003. His free verse, **Brain Storms: A Collection of Free Verse** published in 2005, reflect upon aspects of his bucolic life and his acknowledgement of aging. A cycle of poems: **Thoughts of an Aging Mind**, expressing his frustration with modernity, his acknowledgement of aging and the realization of the impending end of life in more dark rhyme was published in 2008.

Over the years, he has written humorous short stories about the animals in his life. **Pat my Fanny,** stories about the dogs in his life, was published in 2006. **All Critters Big and Little,** is a series of vignettes of his experiences with several creatures that graced his life was published in 2007. His writing encompasses short stories, essays and even children's stories.

About the cover:

    The cover photo was taken by amateur photographer Thomas Fisher. Thomas is a sixteen years old home schooled junior currently accumulating credits towards his college degree in communications while he finishes up high school. Photography naturally blends Thomas' creative talents with his interest in technology. He has been actively learning the art of photography since March 2009.

    One afternoon two stray kittens wandered into a nearby wood near Thomas' home. Both kittens were quickly adopted by his family. "Licorice" the cat that appears in the photo and her sister "Bubbles" still live with Thomas and his family today. To see the full range of Thomas' creative photography visit his website: www.thomasflight.net. You can order prints of this, or any of the other photos on his website by emailing him at: info@thomasflight.net.

The Neighborhood Bully

No one likes a bully. I should, I suppose, qualify that by saying no one likes a bully but his immediate friends, benefactors and, of course, his mom and dad. While all the rest of the world would gladly commute his black heart to Hades, his mom and dad probably have an array of rectangular and oval angelic photographs of the local monster adorning their living room and bedroom as shrines to their love and devotion. Such is the essence of familial myopia.

Growing up in inner city Baltimore during the 40's, we had our share of neighborhood bullies. Given the working class row house structure of tiny blocks, there were many neighborhoods and, of course, many bullies per square mile. As a sub-teen, jaunts to the store or to school were like safaris. They were fearful treks through an array of dangerous lairs of real and imagined bullies. When you're four and a half, an ill tempered, overly hormoned five year old complete with his gang of sycophants is a terrifying obstacle to childhood development. Whimpering, begging, and saying "uncle" to your fellow citizens does not go far in developing your ego, pain not withstanding.

You say your dad is going to Vietnam! Big deal! Heck, I've got to cross 38th Street to get to school. Besides, he at least has a gun and a gang with him. War is, after all, where you find it.

1

Fortunately, most of the bullies didn't materialize on each and every trip. Most days passed with merely a stiff shot of adrenaline to mark their passing. Some neighborhoods boasted of bullies never seen. Only tales of their size and ferocity persisted to put fear and trepidation in young hearts. This made them real. It was far more plausible to us young boys then tales of fairies dancing on moss that the silly neighborhood girls believed. In the inner city, dungeons and dragons were far more real than fairy godmothers and knights in shining armor. Man's mythology is not a product of the ancient world alone.

Bully is a generic term. I suppose it is not the exclusive domain of Homo sapiens. Now that dogs and pussycats have joined us in our creation of a world culture, it was only fitting that they too establish their niche in the world, good or bad.

I'm embarrassed to say, we are the doting stepparents of our neighborhood bully. At first, we could not possibly entertain the thought that our cute, cuddly, soft, fuzzy, lily white, little "Bob" cat could have a "bully-like" bone in his body. How could our cute little pussycat inspire terror in our housing development between our neighbor's dog and catdom? He was the idyllic "child" who rubbed up against us, lay in our laps, and purred his domestication to those who would hear. We, of course, rejected the accusations and hearsay evidence that began to filter back

2

through well meaning friends and neighbors. What parent wouldn't?

He would sometimes come home with obvious marks of combat: a slight blood spot, a nipped ear, a limp. We naturally assumed that he sustained these feline boo boos in a desperate but heroic defense of his personal honor from other marauding bullies. Bob was an altered male. Eunuchs are not known for aggression. He had no . . . Well, let's just say he had no whatever is associated with aggression. Bob was, after all, white; the very symbol of purity and innocence. If he was a black cat, possibly; or even a yellow tiger type then possibly. What's the saying about a book and its cover? Surely it must have been the other kid's fault.

It is true that we were aware of his precociousness in regard to dogs. Bob harassed the local dogs. There was not a dog under three times his size that didn't pass by cautiously, run away from or avoid his presence altogether. Actually, there was one. Just across the street there was an enormous black, pit bull type that moved after some time. He was easily five times Bob's mass. The dog quickly became a pariah by biting the neighbor's cute little cocker spaniel and was relegated to a life on a chain. Bob would deliberately go to within a foot or so of the dog who would bark and thrash about on the end of the chain. He was so frantic with rage that he would choke himself into froth and bark until he was hoarse. Oh how he hated Bob!

3

Bob, on the other hand, would just sit there, mere inches away from catastrophe, and watch. Sometimes, he would even lie down and casually roll over. This would only enrage the dog to even more frothing and choking and gasping. It was the height of insult. No doubt, it was animaldom's equivalent of the finger.

Bob would leave the comfort of a chair in the house just to give chase to a dog that may have been just passing through the neighborhood. For a eunuch cat that had no unmentionables, he sure acted like he had them. But cats chasing dogs is like rabbits chasing hunters. Surely this is not being a bully. The underdog, or undercat in this instance, is greatly admired.

One day he came home highly agitated and nearly covered with blood. Not his blood I must add. "Perhaps he killed a bird or a rabbit" my wife bemoaned. We had already accepted his hunting prowess.

In true human manner, we were schizophrenic in regard to animaldom. Bob would regularly leave dead birds on our doorstep for which we would feel compelled to bury in a ceremonious manner, complete with remorse. The murderer always avoided these ceremonies. He knew that we humans would be out of sorts during the festivities and would be somewhat short with him. He also knew that his food dish would be filled and that we would pet him shortly after.

Humans are weird. What other species of animal would set out a bird feeder and harbor a pussycat at the same time? We put a bright red collar with some bells on Bob to make his presence known to some poor, unsuspecting victim of feline instinct. Also, we religiously filled the bird feeder even though the more exotic birds such as the cardinals and orioles no longer visited our humble offering. Only the blue jays and the mocking birds visited our house. I'm not completely sure that they didn't come just to "rattle" Bob. Blue jays and mocking birds are the bullies of birddom. A cat is fair game to them. Bob apparently had not killed a bird. Perhaps it was a poor bunny. Oh, the infamy!

The next day, we learned that the cute little cat down the street was taken to the hospital and had several stitches in her head. It seems that Bob was less of a gentleman and more of a brute than imagined. In no time, we heard of many tales of bullying and bravado. How embarrassing! We felt compelled to apologize to our neighbor and pay for the veterinary bills. They graciously accepted the former and declined the latter. That made us feel even worse. Once sensitized to the realization that our son may be a bully, we quickly learned that the horrible tales were true. Our innocent child was an ogre.

We soon learned that there was not a cat in the neighborhood that didn't run from or give way to our Bob. Late at night my wife and I became attuned to hearing the meowing and thrashing of cats in combat; and cast knowing glances at one another as to who would initiate the apology to one of our neighbors in the morning. We were rapidly becoming the social outcasts of the neighborhood. No one wanted to be the first to openly declare that our stepchild was a rotten little hoodlum, no matter how cute.

The clincher struck home when some neighbors had a family gathering. People were all over the place. No one knew the next. My wife and I were working outside in the adjacent yard. Bob came ambling down the street. Being a cute little devil, some of the cat loving party guests exclaimed: "Oh look at the pretty kitty. Here kitty, kitty!"

From another part of the teeming masses came the exclamation: "You'd better leave him alone! He's a killer."

Now that hurt. My child a killer? Never! But alas, 'tis true. Bob is a bully. My rectangular and oval pictures in the living room and the bedroom belie the truth. We endure the shame. Like all parents, we hate the sin but love the sinner. He's still our little pussycat.

Bugger

Cats are, by nature, hunters. They hunt anything that moves, be it Cape buffalo, deer, lambs, or field mice. Match their size to the game, and they will stalk and pounce on it. A dust bunny blowing in the wind will cause a nursing kitten to get big eyed, dig in its paws and pounce. That's the way God made them whether we admire it or not. With this in mind, I've never taken the self-righteous position of calling cats cruel. While I may recoil at seeing a lion pull down a young gazelle, I understand that they're just "doing their thing." These same attributes practiced with a ball of yarn or string is invariably called cute.

Bob White, so named lastly for his color and firstly for his Sesame Street namesake, came into my life in "my latter years." Bob and my fiftieth birthday were coincidental. He was a "pound" cat; purchased for the outrageous "donation" of three dollars. I had never paid for a cat in my life. He was a discarded orphan from the urbanized human world. As was relayed to us, his former owners (if one can own a cat) were an elderly couple that became too incapacitated to keep him. This sounded as plausible as a car having been driven by a little old lady who only went to Sunday school.

It must have been so, however, because it became obvious from the start that Bob had never been out of doors. Watching him discover this whole new natural dimension was enjoyable. Behind our cookie cutter suburban house was a cookie size lot. It couldn't have been much larger than a tennis court. But to Bob, it was a new planet; complete with trees, bushes, grass, jungle, savanna, and veldt. Naturally, such an environment attracts all manner of game: birds, squirrels and, of course, bugs.

Bob was good company for our young late life son, which was our reason to get a late life cat. After Bob became acclimated to the household, he became quite a talker. In fact, he had a most grating meow that he used to communicate with his humans. Invariably, his day started at five o'clock in the morning. As with most egocentrics, he felt that if he were up, everyone should be up. At this ungodly hour, he would walk on us and meow loudly. If a couple of meows didn't do it, he would put his face in mine and push with his nose, followed by a well pitched meow right in my ear canal.

After several nights of abbreviated sleep, the old "put the cat out for the night" routine was tried. The problem with this strategy is the dichotomy of hot and cold. If the night was cold, the family would react to my late evening "kitty, kitty" as if I were the Marquis De Sade. My family and love life suffered on cold nights. On hot nights, the windows were left open. At five in the morning, Bob would stand outside my bedroom window and give good imitations of Enrico Caruso with a sore throat. Fearing the wrath of my neighbors and the alienation of my family, a compromise was reached. Bob was put in the basement for the night; that is, those nights that he acquiesced to go to the basement. I was no longer the king of my castle. I was a constitutional monarch at best. At least there were sufficient walls and doors between Bob and me that his five o'clock reminders were not heard.

Bob was a young, altered male with a good disposition and a neurotic tendency to think of himself, on occasion, as a human. Usually, only dogs resort to this unrealistic appraisal of their existence. Cats are normally more psychologically stable. As some people are cat people, I suppose there must be some cats that are people cats. Both have lost their sense of objectivity. As was stated, Bob was altered. This is a pleasant human euphemism for him being castrated. Poor Bob was a eunuch. It probably contributed to his pleasant disposition and gentleness; but not being a cat person and having been branded as one of those disgusting macho red necks, to me, let's face it, Bob was a whoose!

When it came to his newly found world of motion and shadow, however, he became a cat. He was a hunter. At first he pounced upon everything that moved: leaves blowing in the wind; moving blades of grass; birds, although the frontal assault was never successful; shadows of birds and airplanes that crossed his iris, and much more. As the final phrase of an auction ad states: too numerous to mention. A hunter he was by instinct; and a hunter he became through practice.

Unfortunately for the suburbs, the Cape buffalo, deer, lambs, and even the field mice have left for less "busy" pastures. What remains of huntable game is severely limited. Only the uncatchable birds and squirrels remain. Squirrels are not necessarily uncatchable; they are just,

9

well, ugh! . . too darn big. The hunting instinct doesn't justify a painful attack on one of those toothy critters that holds his ground, especially when a can of delicious "Pussy Good Cat Food" is back at the house there for the meowing.

There are bugs, of course. Depending upon the neighborhood, even these are limited in number and variety. But to a true hunter, they are fair game. They move.

A hunter hunts what he can. As there are deer hunters, rabbit hunters, buffalo hunters, etc., Bob was a bug hunter; as I cynically dubbed him: a bugger. He perfected his hunting skills on all manner of bugs. As most practical learning experiences are painful, so too was Bob's early education. One of his early hunts, after discovering his new talent, was a wasp. All other bugs, to date, had fallen under his lightning paws. They never fought back. Before I could intercede in what I knew to be the inevitable, the inevitable happened. He jumped several feet up and backwards at the same time. With a mere wave at his sore paw, he resumed the hunt; now a little wiser in his choice of game. Life has these little setbacks.

We were living in a brand new house. Bulldozers and paving machines had disrupted the former territorial boundaries of the resident animal life. The establishment of territorial rights between humans and the refugee insects had still not been established. Ants and crickets became illegal aliens in what was formerly their nation state. A sort of Palestinian crisis existed

10

in the household: the former dispossessed made frequent raids upon the new titleholders to return to their native space and to show their resolve. They were promptly crushed. Not with malice, mind you, but for lack of better communications. I would have recognized their right of existence if they would have recognized mine. There must be an analogy here somewhere. In any case, Bob became a warrior in this conflict.

Casualties began to appear. Dead and dying ants were found on the kitchen floor. If it moved, it was pounced upon. His greatest triumphs were his nocturnal hunts in the basement. Cricket carcasses began to accumulate at the foot of the stairs. This made my wife rather happy. She was convinced that crickets chewed holes in wool. Their high frequency caterwauling was both annoying and threatening. It is difficult for me to hold a grudge against crickets. Any friend of Jiminy is a friend of mine. To Bob, they were just moving targets.

The ubiquitous bug made Bob's life outside a continual contest. Once past the door, no casual task in itself, he went from adventure to adventure. The quarry was invisible to me, but his gestures showed that he was on the hunt: long slinking crouches here, leaping attacks there. He could be casually walking across the lawn and in the next instant slashing the air to intercept a disturbed beetle. It is amazing how adept he was in the world of the diminutive.

One sultry summer's night between fitful sleep and a disturbing noise in the distance, I had occasion to get up and look out my bedroom window at about three AM. Sultry summer nights have vitality that few humans aside from newspaper boys, milkmen and early rising fishermen are aware. Most people think the world ceases conscious life activities until two hours after sunrise. Nothing could be farther from the truth. One can sense the growing and the moving of unseen things in the darkness. Noises that would never be heard during daylight hours seem to become evident. A whole new world of sound occurs between midnight and sunrise.

It was one of those evenings when Bob had managed to time his late evening romp in the boonies so as to be unavailable when I went to bed. He was left outside in these cases. As I looked out the window into the night, I saw Bob walking across the street from a tour of inspection of my neighbor's property. A municipal mercury vapor street lamp illuminated the yard sufficient to transform Bob's white fur to iridescence. From a casual saunter, he suddenly broke into a wildly, thrashing leap. For nearly two full seconds he was airborne and slashing at a hapless victim. I marveled and envied his senses and physical skills. Cats are natural night hunters.

Not all of Bob's hunting activities were appreciated. That is, at times he created havoc. Bob's fascination with the great out of doors required him to be a great window looker-outer. When he was inside, he would spend a great deal of time watching the coming and goings of the world through the windows. He had no favorite. He made the household tour and stopped at whatever one he found interesting. They must have been good viewing stations. He had, on occasion, actually come in from the outside to set up a vigil at some window. We were always careful to keep the screens down on the second floor windows. He had a habit of leaping from the beds to the windows and using the screens as a runaway buffer to check his forward motion. We lived in fear that one day he would make his accustomed leap into the window and keep right on going.

Windows look like natural escapes to insects. A fly frantically trying to continue his normal flight against a window is a common sight. Flies are common sights. Like the common cold, the common housefly is everywhere. Some bugs have social stigmas. One does not expect to find cockroaches and silverfish in Beverly Hills or Marina Del Rey. I'll bet flies are there. Flies were in our windows, also, from time to time. Their aerial antics were sheer fascination and challenge for Bob. He dispatched quite a few. Not that we objected to the loss of our flies, mind you. It was that in his exuberance of the hunt, he shredded the lacy curtains with his clawed slashings. After a month of hunting, Bob had our home looking very un Beverly Hillish. I suppose that if there is a "Jones" to keep up with in the neighborhood, there has to be a slob that everyone can rise above. In a perverted sort of way, we had a purpose in life. Bob contributed to that image. What could we expect? He was just "doing his thing!" He was a bugger.

Cool Cat

Some people are morning people, some people are night people and some people, well . . , they're neither. I am a night person. Or rather, I was a night person before galloping old age whittled off some of my ambition and energy. My most productive time was from 9:00 in the evening until about 1:00 in the morning.

After dinner, I would swing into high gear, and by 9:00, I'd be mentally and physically into a project; whether writing this story or cleaning out a barn. Some cynical reader may, in fact, liken the two endeavors to each other. The only things that early mornings are good for is hunting, fishing and just watching the sunrise; certainly not for going to work or to school.

I got through college and graduate school between 9:00 P.M. and 2:00 A.M. Maybe that is why I didn't set the world on fire when I was in the public schools. My mother always sent me to bed just at my most productive time. I'm glad I wrote this paragraph. I would have never thought up this grand excuse.

My wife, Jo Ann, is one of those "neithers." Not that she doesn't work; she does. It is just that she has no preference for the morning or the evening. On the contrary, mornings and evenings are for her favorite pastime, sleeping. If I get up early to go fishing, she says, "Don't wake me when you get up, it's too early." If I get into a nighttime project, she again hits me with, "Don't wake me when you come in, it's too late." Sleeping is one of her greatest pleasures.

Another of her pleasures is eating. She nibbles. She can consume great quantities of all manner of potato chips, cheese thingies, pastry, ice cream, pies, toaster pop ups, etc., etc., etc. Snacks come in ten-minute waves throughout her day. She is one of those fortunate individuals who were blessed with a bug's metabolic rate. She was one of those girls that, as a teenager, was envied by her female counterparts and admired by the males. I'm sure you remember the type: the slim, peaches and cream skinned high school cheerleader who could wolf down two boxes of malty balls in the movies and have a banana split and a coke for dessert; and never get even the hint of a zit. Jo Ann was one. For the first twenty years of our marriage, she never gained or lost two pounds. It is enough to make one mad.

As a teenager, if I so much as got caught in a Coke's spray, my face would resemble a raisin pie that someone dropped on my mirror. For those girls who wondered what ever happened to those kinds of girls, I can tell you that they stay peaches and cream and slim. Jo Ann has actually improved over the last twenty some years. For those guys who always wondered about what it might have been like to marry one of those high school beauties, I can tell you that a goodly third of my paycheck for the past twenty some odd years has been for malty balls, cokes, banana splits and other assorted snacks.

The nickname I bestowed upon her was "bunny". Not that the reader should inject some sarcastic connotation upon this endearment. I wish it were so. It was only a soft, cuddly term of endearment. It has held true these many years. Her nickname should have been "kitten". Again, soft and cuddly; but in that kittens just eat, sleep and play, it would have been more appropriate.

Our first cat, Gladys, was also a chowhound. We were living in a little farm house in southern Pennsylvania with Gladys, a young beagle hound named Fanny and a collie type pup named Hank, short for Henry the Eighth. At every snack, the animal life came to an intense standstill until the last crumb of food was no longer seen. The dogs would make a frantic, sniffing search for a "just a chance" morsel that might have fallen unseen. Gladys, being small and lower in the pecking order only because of her size, had to resort to stealth and cunning to get her share of the snacks. An unguarded table, a lid left off or a door left ajar could create an "attractive nuisance". Gladys got her share.

One evening, after a baked chicken feast, I started a project in the barn. I can't remember what it was, but it seemed important at the time. Jo Ann cleaned up and at some time after 10:00 P.M., and after several snacks to be sure, the house was battened down and the night-lights set for me. I was just getting rolling.

I remember that it was 2:00 in the morning. I was calling it quits for the day. As I walked into the kitchen, the aroma of the chicken dinner hung heavy on the air. I decided that I was going to have a late night snack. A chicken club sandwich was suggested by my olfactory sense in collusion with my imagination.

I went to the vintage refrigerator and opened it. The refrigerator light was like the sunrise in contrast to the subdued night-light. There, in the middle of a near empty platter of chicken bones was Gladys, still chewing away; but totally unconcerned about my intrusion. I took her from the refrigerator. Her fur was cold, but she didn't seem to be uncomfortable. Needless to say, she didn't leave me enough chicken to make a sandwich. Bologna just doesn't "cut it" when your heart is set on chicken.

The next morning I made some sort of casual joke about what I found in the refrigerator the previous evening. Jo Ann was both amused and a little shocked that it could have happened. We pieced together a plausible scenario to explain the mishap. Jo Ann, in true form, had a snack at about 9:30. Gladys must have jumped in as Jo Ann put the chicken away and was turning away from the refrigerator. Gladys was just being her cunning self.

I often wondered what would have happened if I hadn't decided to have a late night snack. Would Gladys have frozen to death? Would she have suffocated? The big question that I have racked my brains to find an answer to is: How could she see what she was doing when the light went out? She was a real cool cat that night.

Unfit Mother

There are as many different personalities as there are individuals. This statement applies equally well with humans or cats. As there are nice people, so too are there nice cats. As there are rotten people, so too are there rotten cats. I must admit, however, that there seem to be proportionally more rotten people in this world. Gad, I hope I'm not becoming a cat person.

People have certain stereotypical images of certain people in certain roles. For instance, we expect our priests and ministers and other clergy to act with a certain amount of piety and dignity. It comes with the role. Can you even conjure up a vision of a nun elbowing her way to the front of a line and then giving you the finger for complaining? It is beyond our stereotyped imagination; although at this moment there may well be a nun prostrate before Mother Superior confessing that she gave someone the bird.

We expect our doctors to be intellectual and dignified, our policemen to be kind and helpful, although the new television images have shown another side to their role, our nurses to be spiffy clean; our truck drivers Southern red necks; and our mothers reeking of estrogen, ready to smile at her baby or rush into a burning building to save it. We have definite stereotype expectations about mothers. America, apple pie and motherhood are the big three.

When the perverted few violate this sanctified role, their activity makes the pages of the newspaper; the greater the stereotypical disparity, the lower the page number. If it is great enough, it might even be in the *Enquirer*. When a 300-pound mother sells her twin children to buy a cheesecake, it is so repugnant to our expectation of motherhood that it is of *Enquirer* quality.

The first home I bought upon graduating from college was an old country home on four acres, nestled in the rolling hills of Southern Pennsylvania. It was a picturesque farmhouse on the side of one of those hills. Two great Norway spruce trees by the back porch framed the house in near Currier and Ives perfection. My new bride and I began to face the adult world together in this idyllic setting. Like many naive young people, we got pets to screw it all up.

19

As happens in rural America, cats just occur. A casual statement that we would like a cat given to a farmer could inundate you in cats. Barn cats are like fleas in present numbers and in reproductive potential. I have absolutely no recollection of how Gladys came to us; or where she got the name Gladys. Try pronouncing the name Gladys several times. It is a difficult name. No offense to any of my readers, but I thought this a stupid name for a cat. But I was young and in love and the world was new. My wife could have named the cat Ishkabibal for all that I cared. This was the beginning of the "artsy craftsy", "back to the earth" 1960's. We pioneered the sillies, so why not a cat named Gladys?

Gladys came to us as a large kitten. She was jet black with a white star on her chest that shown like a beacon in the dark. On more than one occasion I located her at night by her guiding star. As a full-grown cat, she never got beyond the size of a large kitten. She was the smallest cat I have ever encountered. Her small size didn't seem to affect her performance as a cat, however. She could hold her own with the many dogs and other cats that graced our home during this phase of my life.

As a hunter, she had no peers. One autumn evening, as happens in the country, she caught a glimpse of a transient field mouse making a run for it across the kitchen. I believe it was the first time that she discovered that the little beggars were sharing her abode. With the speed of summer lightning, she interrupted her food begging with the dogs and made pursuit. In a nip and tuck race, the mouse made it to a cold air return. We could hear him bang and clatter for cover amidst the maize of aluminum tunnels in spite of his or her diminutive size. Gladys took point at the air duct and started a mouse watching vigil. This was around six o'clock in the evening.

At ten o'clock, the time I normally put her out for the night, she was still on alert. She was so intent on getting that mouse that I didn't have the heart to break her concentration. I left her there with her eyes starring at the grate, her body at the set and the tip of her tail twitching. She really wanted that mouse.

When I got up to fix coffee the next morning, as was my chore, there was Gladys in the same position and in the same state of readiness. I can only assume that she had spent the entire night ready to pounce on the mouse that, by now, had had a good night's sleep and was probably in the bag of dog food in the basement. Gladys had been "on point" for around twelve hours. I've seen patient hunters, but never one as patient as Gladys.

She was normal in other ways, too. At the appropriate time in her maturation, the neighbor's tomcats began to call, or rather howl. Even our peaceable beagle hounds couldn't stand the racket at ungodly hours and would bark their displeasure. You know how brothers can be about a girl's choice of boyfriends. Her suitors were, without a doubt, the ugliest cats I had ever seen.

The whole bunch of suitors was enormous. I assume they were all brothers. Their fur was reddish brown with black patches. I believe the mixture is peculiar to Brindle Terriers. On Terriers, it looks good. On cats, it looks like hell. Having never had daughters, I can still appreciate the father who opens the door for his daughter's first date and discovers that he has to be nice to something he would have thrown stones at only ten years previously.

As daughters don't listen to the counsel of their wiser fathers, Gladys didn't respond to my attempts to interfere with nature. My very little girl got into a family way. She was so small, I was concerned; but, in fact, she didn't show her pregnancy. As a matter of fact, she didn't take it seriously at all. When the estimated time of arrival had come, my wife had prepared a comfy, padded bed for the nursery. While she introduced Gladys to her creation, Gladys showed no interest. My wife thought that we must have underestimated her "time".

One summer afternoon, my wife and I were home patching up the patches on our vintage house. She was painting on the back porch when she responded to a sound she described as a mouse squealing. Upon an exhaustive ear to wall search, she discovered a bawling, bloody little thing that looked like an overgrown rat baby. On inspection, she realized that it was a kitten. Gladys, we assumed, had given birth to a kitten, but couldn't be bothered beyond the temporary inconvenience of giving birth. The first was between the studs of a wall that was being repaired.

Together, we followed a fading bloody trail. A second squalling brat cat was found in the rainspout of the back porch on which I was working. It was covered with the same bloody goo, well camouflaged with pine needles. We cleaned it up and continued the search for its siblings and its errant mother. We found one more teetering on the back porch windowsill. We found no more kittens. Only Gladys and the Almighty know if any more were discarded that day.

After we found Gladys, she didn't volunteer to nurse the squealing beggars. Only with physical force and prodigious amounts of bribes of all manner of uncatly goodies such as ice cream and my wife's chicken livers could we induce her to allow them to nurse. Fortunately for them and for us, once the milk began to flow, she volunteered to nurse them. I'm sure it was for her personal comfort and not because of any maternal love drive.

Within just a few weeks, the kittens were bigger than Gladys and uglier than their old man; or old men as the case may be. Subsequent litters were somewhat normal, but never maternal. At least, she had them all in one place in future births. It fell to my wife and me to find a place for the nursery after the fact. Gladys never seemed to care where they were placed as long as she didn't have to deal with them beyond the feedings. Gladys fed them and then walked away. We cleaned them up; all eleventy-eleven of her offspring, each bigger and uglier than the next. As can happen in the country, we found foster homes for them all. Barns provide a never-ending funnel for unwanted waifs in the rural areas. Between milk strippings, mice and dry dog food, the cats are reared in those egalitarian socialist orphanages. And, they seem to like the company. I've never heard of a cat running away from a good cattle barn.

Let's face it, as a mother Gladys stunk! She gave motherhood a bad name. Not that some humans don't do the same thing. It's just that we expect more from the lower animals. We certainly don't expect them to sink to our human level. Gads! Maybe I am becoming a cat person. Gladys was just another unfit mother. But, like humans, we loved her in spite of her shortcomings.

Damn the Torpedoes

We of the Western World usually take delight in tracing our culture back to the Ancient Egyptians. If the truth were known, my ancestors were probably Scots who painted their naked bodies blue and frightened the more civilized Ancient Romans into stopping their

Northern campaign at Hadrian's Wall with the realization that the Scots were too barbaric even to make war upon. But, after the Romans became extinct, it was fashionable to claim credit for the fact that the Scots were triumphant over the Romans who were triumphant over the Greeks who were triumphant over the Egyptians. Therefore, in some perverse logic, we have a direct claim to the cultural belly button of European civilization even though each destroyed the other in civilized succession.

Egypt was and is essentially a desert. Life followed the river, but basically, it was dry. It is no wonder, then, that pussycats are found on the drawings of the Ancient tombs of the Egyptians. Pussycats are not kindly disposed toward water. By this, I mean that they are far from amphibious animals. They'll drink it; but given there 'druthers, will have little else to do with it. You have never heard of a cat retrieving a duck, have you? Dogs may take to water, but pussycats will avoid it at all costs.

Cartoon characterizations of Dennis the Menace washing his pet bowser are a stereotypical situation in real life. One can man handle even large dogs into the bathtub. I know of few people who successfully bathe their pussycats on some consistent basis. Even Rambo would have to have a death wish to attempt to manhandle his tiny tabby. Fighting a battalion of Russian Special Forces is child's play in comparison. Having one's skin shredded by a reluctant pussycat is the price one pays for just showing a cat the bath water. It goes downhill from there.

Bob, my present pussy, won't even go outside if it is raining. He will sit at the door and complain in no uncertain meows that he doesn't like rain one darn bit. When he is forced to get his feet wet, he raises each one in succession, stretches it straight out, and shakes it at a speed reminiscent of humming bird wings. You can see the disgust in his expression. Lately, any attempt to eject him into the damp world gives rise to threatening hisses and growls that are supposed to deter me. Only a kick in the butt encourages obedience.

The nearest Bob gets to water is his unorthodox manner of drinking it. We keep a bowl of water in his kitty corner, his spot by the refrigerator; but he rarely drinks from his bowl. For some reason, he drinks from the faucet in the tub. The only time there is water present is immediately after I take a shower. Shortly after I start my morning shower, Bob shows up at the bathroom door and goes through his "let me in" antics. This consists of a rather raucous "meow" followed by his paws poking under the bathroom door to get my attention. On getting out of the shower, he gets in.

As I dry off, he sits at the faucet and drinks as the showerhead drains. I can hear his rough tongue being dragged across the opening. The noise is like fingernails on a chalkboard. It sounds awful; and the pipe, like an old phonograph resonator amplifies the sound throughout the house. Actually, Bob spends a good deal of time in the shower. The devilish side of me would love to squirt him good. One day, he's going to be in there when I hurriedly turn the thing on. So far, he's been darn lucky.

Cats have been transported all over the world by boat; but that doesn't make them mariners at heart. Fortunately, boats are dry. When you see the movies of the steel men in their wooden ships climbing the masts of their sailing ships in the midst of a Nor'easter, you can bet that his pet pussycat is asleep on his bunk. There's no darn way that pussycat would even get on deck much less go up a stupid, slippery rope.

I have a cat person friend that takes canoe trips with her feline companion. Anyone who would name a cat Cassiopeia has got to be a cat person. This act in and of itself does not convince me of the marine nature of the animal. Only when the fuzzy feline dives off the gunwales for a cool dip will I'll be convinced. What are the odds of that happening? Ha!

It isn't as though cats can't swim. They can. As a mean little kid, like most inquisitive little monsters, I have thrown cats into swimming pools, streams, ponds, etc. They always swam with great skill, and always away. Unlike dogs that end their swim with a good shaking, pussycats usually slither off looking remarkably like drowned rats and totally disgusted with their plight and the monster that caused it. I rather like to think of these events as youthful scientific experimentation. They really were. There are probably several hundred pussycats across the nation at this moment that are being tossed into the drink so that some young boy can tell another young boy: "See! I told you so! Cats really can swim". If the cats could talk, they would have some very unkind things to say about the questionable parentage of their dunkers.

On my first "farmette", I had a pond. It was deep enough for all manner of frogs, itinerant snapping turtles, transient ducks, and a few self stocked fish; but not deep enough to go swimming in. Much to the benefit of my neighbor down stream, the pond leaked like a sieve. The muskrats created a virtual sponge out of the earthen dike on its deepest end. My neighbor actually moved his garden to his border with me to take advantage of a natural irrigation system. He had one heck of a garden, I might add. The pond was a giant eye on a whole different world. Summer evenings were dominated by the sounds of frogs and insects that made the pond their noisy residence. It was a grand mud hole.

I also had cats. I had a little hussy, named Gladys that was in some stage of being "knocked up" for the duration of her tenure with us. We always had two or three of her nearly grown children with us at any given time. Her fertility put a great strain on the ability of the neighboring barns to absorb her production. Gladys hated water also.

Because cats are so "water shy", the experience that I had one afternoon was unusual. It was so out of character for the kittens that the event burned into my memory. All of Gladys multitudinous brood liked me for some reason; some more than others. I had a Pied Piper relationship with the cats. They sought me out if I were outside.

I was out walking on my estate in a lord-of-the-manor fashion when I encountered three of Gladys kittens out for an afternoon frog and grasshopper hunt among the tall grasses on the pond's shallows on the opposite side. We exchanged greetings; I with "hello there you ugly little waifs"; they with their diminutive "meows".

Ugly they were. Their daddy was one of several enormous red toms that my gardening neighbor housed in his barn. They were the undisputed lords of the valley. Red appeared in every kitten born in a five mile radius of his barn. Not a brilliant red of a strawberry blonde or the red of an Irish setter. It was always red patches as if black kittens were splashing about in a red paint can. They looked like heck, but they were cute anyway.

All three wanted to join me and I welcomed their company. The distance from me to them was less than a hundred feet around the edge of the pond. One decided that he would take the short cut. With no hesitation, he dove into the water and swam straight toward me. I was shocked. The others, in true cat fashion, made their way around the bank. It was the one and only time that I saw a cat willingly take to water.

Now that it's too late, I wish that I had saved that particular kitten for selective breeding.

29

Maybe I could have bred the first honest to goodness duck retrieving cat. In the great maritime tradition of Admiral Farragut, the cat had a "Damn the torpedoes, full speed ahead" inclination. He was different.

Endearing Young Charms

To own a pussycat is to love a pussycat; if one can own a cat. I've exercised some poetic license to be sure, but my point is made. Pussycats have some very endearing qualities. Given an opportunity, like the Sirens of the Greek myths, they can seduce you with their many charms. We have a litany of clichés concerning charming "catlike" qualities. I find it interesting that they are nearly always applied to women. There must be a psychological message in this somewhere.

Playfulness, for example, is one of a pussycat's endearing charms. While pouncing upon something in motion can be explained as a cat's survival tool; in the human household, it is a source of humor that can turn a dreary or hectic day into an entertaining interlude.

Prior to writing this paragraph, I was putting on my boots. I love great clodhopper boots that are impervious to cold, wet, and stone bruises. They have long strings that securely bind the boots high above the trajectory of the

30

inadvertent pebble that regularly invades the low cut regular shoes. Pebbles cause pain all out of proportion to their diminutive size.

Tying those long strings is a comical chore. It becomes a tug of war between Bob, my errant pussycat, and me; and others before Bob; one loop and another tug of war. The ends of my laces look like limp paintbrushes. The last inch or so have been shredded in fierce combat. I estimate that I get twenty miles to the lace. He must hear my boots squeak when I pick them up because he seems to attack from out of nowhere. Another loop entices yet another bestial attack on an imagined filet mignon of sorts.

The passage of a finger or toe under the bed covers can cause a ferocious attack. At four thirty in the morning, this can be quite sobering; but at other times, it is merely amusing. I love to scratch the bed with the slightest movement and watch the cat pounce with precision. Whether young kitten or old cat, they seem to enjoy the game of "pouncing the finger", or whatever. One needs to be careful of what constitutes the whatever. If I may, in the great scientific tradition of Newton and Murphy, offer a natural law, it is: "Never make love with a cat in the bedroom"! They don't know when the game has ended.

Cats by their physical nature are endearing. For one thing, they have a stoic bearing. They have a way of laying in such a manner that their front "wrists" protrude. I call this their "hatching eggs" stance. No animal seems to have the perfect geometry of line that the cat exhibits. No wonder the sphinx had a cat's body. The ancients admired it also.

Another of the many charms of a pussycat is their tongue. Unlike the elongated, dripping hunk of meat that dominates a dog's profile, the pussycat has a tiny "flickerini" that is rarely seen; except perhaps from genuine pedigree Persian cats who seem to have trouble getting all of their tongue tucked securely back into their pushed-in face. Licking is to pets what hand shaking is to people. Tongues are the tools of self-expression.

Lucy, the famous female character of Peanuts, has an aversion to "dog germs". She reacts negatively to being "kissed" by Snoopy, the ultimate hero and beagle of the bunch. I too have been kissed by beagles as well as a myriad of other breeds of dogs. While I don't have a major aversion to their sloppy expression of endearment, I have on occasion resorted to my handkerchief to consummate their affection. They have dissolved several layers of skin over the years. My anti-dog friends usually grimace in disgust at my tolerance for their disgusting display of affection.

Perhaps Lucy and my anti-dog friends would tolerate a pussycat. Not only are cats infinitely cleaner in body and gesture, they rarely resort to "kissing" as an expressing of love. And when they do, they have a built in towel. Rather than leaving a slimy residue, often with a twinge of what ever they were eating over the last hour as dogs will often do; pussycats will exhibit a nice clean lick. It is like comparing an unwanted passionate French kiss to a formal kiss on the back of the hand.

A cat's tongue is rough. While no doubt no more hygienic than the dog's lick, the impression is one of cleanliness and good taste; that is, on the part of the licker. When they lick, cats and cows seem to actually rasp off a layer or two of skin. It is a strange sensation to the uninitiated. Even the most squeamish among us must admit that a kiss from a pussycat is not the stomach turning experience that they remember from their friend's overly friendly bowser. It is a truly admirable and wholly practical charm.

It is difficult not to admire a true athlete. We humans have a long tradition of honoring athletic prowess. The ancient Greeks seem to have institutionalized athletics. Athletes push the capability of the human body to its extremes. Gymnastics, to me, is the ultimate expression of human movement. The leaping, twisting, turning, and bending of the gymnast show me to what extent I have allowed the good life to impede my movement. My girth alone, not to mention my inactivity, have combined to reduce my motion to a mere forward and backward locomotion. After watching a gymnastics event, I feel more akin to a bopper toy than a human. Fortunately, I can fall back on age as an excuse.

I don't need a steady diet of gymnastics on television. My pussycat provides me with a never-ending source of entertainment. Cats are natural gymnasts. This is another of their endearing charms. Even my Bob, who has visibly indulged in the good life, continues to amaze me in his bodily control. He, like his predecessors, borders on being a contortionist. There is always another shape that he manages to twist his pudgy little self into. Usually, he engages in his gymnastics during his toilette. I realize that this term refers to ladies, but if we can attach catlike behaviors to women, we can attach womanlike behaviors to cats; ergo: cats have toilettes. It sounds more elegant, you must admit!

Other than his face, the top of his head, and his ears, there is no place on his body that he cannot lick with his tongue. This requires some absolutely amazing fetes of agility. Try to imagine licking the back of your thigh. This only requires that you sit on your backbone approximately at the end of your ribs, extend your torso upward and twist it at about 120 degrees. Don't forget to hold your leg up in the air at 75 degrees for a considerable length of time. Nothing to it; right? This is just another of their fascinating charms. If you are disposed to put some fun in your life, get a pussycat. Their endearing charms and feline antics will captivate and entertain you beyond measure.

Fat Cat

The term, fat cat, somehow became lost to the feline world until their mythical champion, Garfield, reinstated it. Its origin is somehow lost to antiquity. Perhaps some enterprising Ph.D. candidate in English will research its origin and launch a lifetime government grant to pursue the ramifications of this important contribution to man's cultural heritage; leaving the more mundane chores of keeping the system working to us less important beings. He or she may, if the government is generous enough, become one him or herself.

While the origin may be obscured, the meaning is crystal clear. We know one when we see one. How one gets to be one, whether human or feline, is pretty much the same: an excess of the good life! Cat people, the term I use for those people who love cats as privileged equals rather than as pets, often provide this good life. My mother and my younger brother were two such cat people.

Sometime after I left home as an independent adult, the vacant niche in my mother's household was filled by a silky black female cat with a gentle disposition. To eliminate the Freudian complications with a perfect daughter and to increase her gentleness, she was altered. This is a cat person's polite way of saying that her kitty making apparatus was removed. It happened while she was still quite young. With all the tenderness that I can't recall ever expended upon me, my mother nursed her back to normalcy. All the youthful energy that would have gone into the feminine mystique went into flab. Samantha, as my little brother dubbed her, grew to enormous proportions. She became, with the aid of the good life, a fat cat.

I disclaim any influence or even of having knowledge of the early pampering of Samantha. Only on rare occasions did I make the pilgrimage back to the home of my misspent youth. I was too busy making my way in the adult world and misspending that. Telltale indications of the degree to which my mother had become a cat person were evident now with hind sight.

As I did in my adolescence, I took the liberty of making forays to the family refrigerator for a morsel of food, more recreational than nutritional. Whenever I opened the door, two penetrating green eyes would greet me as if she was the official keeper of the refrigerator. Actually, more like the Vestal Virgin to the great white god. Where most cats will rub across a human's legs to induce food to appear, Samantha rubbed the refrigerator. Like Aladdin, she rubbed her magic food chest and made a wish, actually many. If a cat person were a witness to this adoration to her god, goodies would spew forth in gargantuan amounts. God is great. God is good. Let us thank it for this food!

Over the years, as happens to most religious shrines, the over zealous believers cause some damage. Samantha actually wore off the enamel finish at the base of the door. To this day, the refrigerator is still functional as a secondary beer cooler; but bald.

Sixth and even seventh senses are attributed to cats. I for one believe in the operation of senses beyond the human experience. As science has been able to identify and quantify infrared and ultrasonic senses in some animals, there is no reason to preclude a whole range of extra sensory capabilities in many of the familiar animals. Cats, I'm convinced have a unique ultra goodies sense.

Samantha, or just Sam to family members, could be nowhere in sight or, in what I considered to be, in earshot of my activities. The slightest sound of a food can being bumped, or an opening kitchen cabinet or, even more eerie, just handling the can opener would cause Sam to appear as if conjured by the food genie or by the Wicked Witch of the Garbage Can. This phenomenon occurred far too methodically to be explained by mere sensory chance, at least by the normal senses.

When Sam made her appearance, it was an event. She was an enormous cat, possibly topping twenty pounds. That's as large as a bag of groceries; and, come to think of it, roughly the same composition. For those of you who have no sense of proportion, that is the size of a small cocker spaniel. She was iridescent black with large green eyes. To have those eyes suddenly peer at you from seemingly out of nowhere could give you quite a start. If you had a bad heart, it could give you quite a stop, if you'll allow my pun. She was massive. There was a fold of skin that hung down from her hind legs to her front legs along each of her sides. I've noticed it only on the big cats such as lions and tigers and especially on the American puma. For some reason, it was on Sam. The food must have met her vitamin needs; and then some. Her fur was glossy and soft. She was pretty to look at, although obviously fat.

It wasn't as though Sam was a chowhound, mind you. Actually, she was more finicky than that great star of television advertising, Morris. It was just that she was persistent in a household of cat people in the midst of affluence. Sam was the embodiment of the good life gone into calories. She consumed a full can of prepared cat chow at a feeding. Feedings occurred nearly every time someone went into or near the kitchen. My guess is that each member of the family gave Sam three meals a day. That is three persons plus transients, times three. Let's say, in round numbers, ten feedings a day. That doesn't include the bowl of dry cat food kept constantly filled as a snack dish; nor the scraps from pre and post breakfast, lunch, dinner and snacks from the human feedings.

For some strange reason, cats and dogs like me. My wife cynically suggests that we are mental equals; and they immediately perceive a fellow pea brain with which to identify. I, of course, reject this scurrilous attack on my I.Q.; but, embarrassingly, can't come up with a more acceptable explanation. If I go into a strange house, the owner's cat will eventually end up on my lap; often to the amazement of the owner. Samantha, being of comparable mental parity, showed her affection for me. The problem was that when she jumped into my lap, I winced in pain and talked an octave higher for the next hour. When she jumped on you; you knew it.

I had an eccentric aunt who was a genuine cat person's cat person. She made her living with cats. She ran a nationally know "cattery" of purebred Persian cats complete with faces that looked as though they ran sixty mile an hour into a brick wall nose first. As my mother's older sister, she felt compelled to tell my mother what to do and what to think. This big sister syndrome naturally carried over to all the lesser beings in my mother's sphere of influence. This meant every one in my family. As I grew older, I naturally rebelled against this intrusion into my personal thinking process. My aunt never forgave me and eventually ostracized me. Somewhere, I have a first cousin my age that I wouldn't recognize if I fell over her.

My aunt's decrees were passed along to me by rote memory incantations. One of which was: "You're going to kill that cat by feeding her so much." Sure enough, Sam died of what I believe to have been a heart attack due to excessive exertion and overweight. Of course, it was at the ripe old age of twenty. She looked as fat, black and silky at the time of her death as she did when she was a kitten. I don't think any of my aunt's pampered and dietetically controlled pansy cats ever saw fifteen. My mother often quoted her German foster mother: "A fat baby is a healthy baby". Maybe it works with cats as well. Sam was definitely a fat cat.

Fight or Flight?

All animals have the reputation of fighting when they are cornered. Even the tiny shrew is said to be a vicious fighter if it is forced to. I've witnessed quite a few valiant "back to the wall" stands by a variety of animals. Even a ferocious house mouse once put on rather dramatic act of bravado and finally attacked my shoe. I was so impressed with his courage that I spared his life and transported him to my barn where he had a second chance and his daring act would be more useful.

I've seen many pussycats with their chance for flight blocked suddenly turn and take a stand. This characteristic fighting stance is theatrical. They arch their backs and raise the hair on their tail. Now I'm sure there is a scientific reason for this pose. I'm guessing that the arched back creates a smaller target and the flared tail exaggerates the cat's size. Not having a tail, I just can't imagine what it would be like to control the tail hairs. Would it be like raising the proverbial hairs on the back of your neck all the way down to your bum and beyond? I wonder if they have any control on the process at all. It's quite impressive with the pussycats.

Kittens nearly double their size. Just two days before this writing, I was walking along a city street where I accidentally kicked a large stone that took off soccer ball fashion across the sidewalk. Amid the general noise of cars, trucks and people, it was an inconsequential addition to the din; except to a longhaired, rusty red kitten that was in a driveway. It was definitely a part of his world. As I strolled by, he was in his fighting, "hold that line" stance. The stone must have made a threatening sound at his level of reality. Not knowing what or where it was caused him to take his fight pose. Flight was impossible without a definite avenue of escape. He was 50 percent tail, 50 percent confused and 100 percent bluff.

In spite of all the pictures I've seen of the great cats holding their own against packs of hound dogs, hoards of natives, and even herds of elephants; my feeling is that most of the drawings are so much imagined "bull". My experience with their little cousins is that, given the slightest opportunity, they'll run like the proverbial "bat out of hell". One of the most successful survival skills of the cat family is that they resort to flight. There is a thin line between bravery and stupidity. I've never seen a stupid pussycat. Maybe that is why a recent study found that pussycats are the most numerous pet in America. On a planet where the dominant animal is not feline, you don't get to be number two by being stupid. There is something to be said of flight.

At my decrepit age, I look back with amazement at how few times the human animal is really frightened. I don't mean startled at the unexpected hand that grabs the heroine in a movie plot or the sudden alarm like noise of a bad door seal on a jet airplane at 35,000 feet. I mean real fear such as the first time, as a teenage Adonis, you stick your foot in your mouth and challenge the supremacy of the reigning bull(y); or the first time, as a teenage soldier, you come under fire in war. It makes you feel like you are an unwilling passenger inside your body. The entire objective world seems to relish a good bloodletting. Fear is a lonely feeling. Flight is a heck of a sight better than fright; but there are times in a man's life where he must just rise above panic and consciously take a stand.

The human female seems to avoid even these foolhardy rites of passage. After a couple of wives, many secretaries, and a lifetime of observation, it appears that women live in a state of constant startle. "Oh! You frightened me!" as I walk into my office and say "Good morning". "Oh! You frightened me!" as I walk into my bedroom. "Oh! I didn't expect anyone to be there!" as I enter my own home at the end of the day. I'm convinced that nature has endowed the human female with a lower threshold of fright than the male; but has developed a system whereby the male of the species has to stand and fight while the female grabs the kids and runs. I suppose it works well for the survival of the species. The fight or flight syndrome was designed by someone a lot smarter than me.

As a youngster, I delivered newspapers at absurdly early hours of the morning. At four o'clock in the morning, it is a lonely and frightening world. In the far gentler world of my youth, the hobgoblins of the imagination were more prevalent than any real threat. Egalitarianism and a concern for civil rights had not as yet flooded the city streets with weirdoes and dangerous "fellow Americans"; nor had the Great Society provided them with the economic capabilities to extend their threat to the suburbs. The only thing we had to fear was fear itself. Maybe fear is just a device to keep the organism "on its toes".

Much of my paper route had apartment houses that were built after World War II. They were, by today's standards, very well built; but designed in the manner of World War II military barracks and defense plant housing. Thousands of buildings looking identical to one another and housing four or more families were the rage and necessity of the time. Fortunately, they all had lights in the entry that were illuminated until dawn. The only problem that I encountered was that there was a short period of a couple of weeks in the early spring when dawn didn't coincide with daylight saving's time. The hall lights were set to turn off at about four thirty A.M. Normally, at four thirty, the sky is illuminated with the promise of the coming sun, sufficient to navigate by. When society shifted from standard time to daylight saving's time, the spring sun was still too far below the horizon to do justice to the morning sky. For several weeks until the sun moved its way north, at four thirty, the mindless hall lights went out and my paper route and my world became dark and fearful.

Suspicious and concerned that the bogeyman was going to grab me in the dark, I floundered around in the black halls, often making blustery noises of bravado that I'm sure the sleeping recipients of my newspapers didn't appreciate at that time of the morning. Probably, to this day, there are some people who think back and tell their spouses that they never got a good night's sleep when they lived at that apartment for some reason or another. Sorry! I may have been the reason, but was long gone before you realized what might have disturbed your sleep. Making a lot of noise can sometimes allay fear. Julie Andrews in The Sound of Music whistled a happy tune. I just thrashed about sounding like a large rampaging bull. Nature's rule of thumb is: "When you can't run, make a lot of noise".

One morning during this transition time, fate conspired to arrange events so that I had an experience that I shall neither forget nor explain for the duration of my life. This particular morning, my usual gang of transient, friendly canine vagabonds that were my normal companions did not accompany me. For some strange reason, I was all alone. As I fumbled my way into the ink black darkness of an apartment building, the hobgoblins of my mind took tangible form. As I felt along the stairwell, something jumped on my shoulders and screamed. Darkness is not man's domain. Not fully remembering what I did, I returned the warrior's cry, thrashed about and freed myself from my attacker. After the fact, I realized that I had been attacked, leopard fashion, by a pussycat. How he got into the apartment was a mystery. Why he attacked me in such a heroic manner is beyond me. He darted out of the building when I made my hasty exit.

To this day I can't explain the circumstances. Some kids probably put the poor cat in the hallway as a nighttime prank. The cat, no doubt, became frightened when he realized that he was trapped. I was, no doubt, the first creature to interrupt his mental hobgoblins. Somehow, our paths crossed. Did he feel compelled to fight when flight was impossible? Was it a legitimate attack or was I just in the way? Was it fight or flight?

The Fish Eater

There is a definite difference between cats and dogs. Now there's a brilliant statement! By this I mean that, at least for me, there is little similarity in the way humans interface with them. From their entry to their demise, a whole series of definite cat activities or definite dog activities dominates the relationship. If this were not so, I suppose there wouldn't be those who love one and hate the other; or it wouldn't make a difference whether one owned a cat or dog. The well rounded of us owns at least one of each. My high point, or my low point, depending upon one's point of view, was twenty-one dogs and seven cats. No disparity intended. Rural beagles are more prolific than rural cats. But that is another story. A study of this relationship would be most interesting; especially to the marketing industry. I'm sure salesmen have a number of insights into this relationship.

One example of this difference is the way dogs or cats come into one's life. For the modern urbanite, dogs come to them in the same manner that they get their toys or videotapes. They go to the mall, browse among the bejeweled centrifugal bumble puppies, get caught by the hype or the point of purchase gimmicks and buy one. If you don't believe me, go to your friendly shopping mall anywhere in this land and see if it has a pet store with a never ending supply of smiling gawkers observing the stock of AKC registered charmers. Unlike the high pressure salesmen in the other stores, when their wares' big brown eyes meet the prospective customer's eyes, a stream of near nauseating ohhs! and awes! comes naturally. Dog owners are soft touches.

Cats, on the other hand, don't enter the scenario in quite the same way. That same pet store may have a few kittens available, but they are always in the last cage or in a spare aquarium set aside from the main sales pitch. Cats still suffer from a smear campaign that started in medieval times. The press never printed a retraction. On Halloween, you never see a picture of a witch flying through the sky on a broom with a beagle on the back, ears flapping in the breeze. It is difficult to imagine a scene in which a witch is pouring a disgusting goo into a cauldron; and rather than having a black cat patiently watching, having a redbone hound lap up the mess when the witch wasn't looking. Dogs don't have a connotation of evil or intrigue. They're too stupid for that role.

With the exception of the upper crust and cat people who get fancy cats from registered "catteries", most cats start from hand written signs on cardboard which state: "Free kittens". Some kittens show up in the arms of preschoolers who shock the unsuspecting parent with "can I keep it?" A dispossessed full-grown cat is doomed. In the rural areas, cats just arrive; mostly through fertility and migration. What's one or half dozen more barn cats? With the exception of a late life addition to my family to amuse a late life human addition to my family, I personally never went to get any of the many cats that passed through my life. They just arrived one day or were thrust upon my good nature. A good example of this was how Amos came into my life.

My wife and I were at our summer camp. Before your mind leaps ahead and visions of a posh log cabin snuggled amid the pristine hills comes to mind, let me say that we had a broken down old farmhouse with no "conveniences" that I bought as a hunting camp in North -central Pennsylvania. We had neighbors. Like-minded people tend to do similar things.

One evening, while sitting on our back porch having coffee with our neighbors, their brother and sister-in-law drove up and joined us. It seemed that economic misfortune was causing them to lose their apartment and that they had to find a "temporary" home for their cat. Amos was a very young strawberry blonde tiger tom with a pleasant disposition. In that it was still summer, they wanted to just leave him at our camp. The argument was that he would stick around and could fend for himself until they could reclaim him. Besides, we came to camp every weekend and they were around periodically; he would be all right. One cup of coffee later, my wife and I were alone with a new cat acquisition; still wondering how it happened. We wanted a cat about as much as we wanted a headache; the latter being the more desirable.

We had no cat food. The nearest food store was some thirty miles in the wrong direction and was closed to boot. Cats are resourceful and independent; but Amos was still very much a kitten. I had to improvise. What did we have to feed him? Our larder, hasty weekend instant food fare, was exhausted. We had a stream behind the camp. In the spring, it was a renowned trout stream. At this time of year, it was low and too warm for the trout that managed relief by finding refuge in colder feeder streams or the lake downstream. The stream was still loaded with fallfish, a term loosely applied to the dace family, a sort of overgrown minnow. Why not catch a few fallfish for Amos. Don't cats like fish? Is there a cat cartoon that doesn't extol the feline love for fish? What a grand excuse to go fishing.

In no time with the aid of my trusty fly rod and a light Cahill dry fly, a six-inch fall fish was flopping madly at Amos' feet. Like any good cat, he pounced and polished it off in no time; bones crunching to nothingness. As fast as I caught them, he consumed them. We were a feeding team; both enjoying our respective roles.

All good things must come to an end and we had to leave. A twang of guilt began to grow in us. What the heck! Amos wasn't our cat. They asked if he could stay there. Well! He was going to stay there and fend for himself. I was an old country boy, wasn't I? Cats are cats. I wasn't encumbered with all those silly cityfied pet hang-ups. Amos would be all right. Country cats are not like those pampered city pet pussies. I did leave a substantial cache of fallfish for him just in case, however.

It was a four-hour drive back to the big city. If my wife, Jo Ann, asked me once, she asked two hundred times: "Are you sure he'll be all right?"

"Of course, he'll be all right." I lied. How the heck could I know whether he'd be all right? While cats are "cool"; some of them can be stupid. In my experience, cats really don't need people. Amos may not hang around for long, but he'd survive. The die was cast.

For one entire week, the whereabouts and fortune of Amos hung over our household like a pending court sentence. Jo Ann's overprotective cityfied blubberings began to affect my heart of stone. I began to have misgivings over my judgment of a cat's survivability. By the next weekend, the four-hour drive to the mountains seemed to take slightly under a year and a half. We arrived sometime after dark and called for Amos. "Here Amos!" "Here Kitty!"

No Amos! The "I told you so"'s came like the judge's verdict from my wife. "We shouldn't have left him here all by himself."

Suddenly, the whole episode became my fault. I was an ogre in my wife's opinion. "Maybe the neighbors picked him up," I countered. "Maybe he went downstream to the next camp. Maybe a friendly cat-loving fisherman picked him up and took him home. Maybe . . ad nauseam". Why should I take all the blame? Too late now, I rationalized. He wasn't our cat, anyway. I was here for the fishing, not to do penance.

Night fishing along the creek is a lot of fun. While you catch mostly junk fish, the ones you catch are huge. With a degree of hurt pride, a twinge of hopefulness and a chance to get away from my wife's self righteous haranguing, I took my gear and went to the stream. With my flashlight, I searched the banks. Nothing moving! "Here Amos!" Blackness! Only the sound of the stream flowing over the exposed rocks could be heard. What the heck!

On the first cast, a huge suckerfish made the water explode. He must have gone three pounds and eighteen inches. Alas, if it were only a trout. There are no olive wreathe crowns for suckerfish catchers. You don't even mention that you catch them to the potbelly stove crowd much less describe their size. It was something to take my mind off my misjudgment. My male ego had taken a shellacking that night. Why women think that their husbands who are about the same age and have the same schooling should be all wise and all knowing about all things is a burden too great to bear at times.

From somewhere along the pitch-black stream bank I heard something. Was it a deer? Was it a raccoon? It sounded like a "meow." Sure enough! In the beam of the flashlight stood Amos. I caught a small sucker at the same time and tossed it to him. He wolfed it, or should I say lioned it, down and waited for more. I happily obliged. I'm sure he was no happier to see me than I him. He had restored my faith in male superiority. I could again face my wife with a subtle: "You doubted me?" The young fish eater had returned.

Amos ate much better after that. The next day I drove the thirty some miles in the wrong direction to satiate my feeling of guilt. The neighbor's in laws never made claim to Amos. Amos returned with us and became a city cat with a life that belied his rural origin. The fish eater became our cat; or rather we became his people.

The Old Watering Hole

The story of the wild cats in Africa seems to revolve around the various watering holes that pockmark the savannas. Every animal on the plains seems to make their wary weary way to the water hole. Water is the sine qua none of life; the common denominator. Whether man or beast, water is the essential around which life revolves. If it were not for water, the coffee bean may never have formed a solution that launched the human animal on his quest to transform the Garden of Eden into the Bronx.

While we civilized humans, the paragon of animals according to Shakespeare, have modified the old water hole into two spigots and a handle; the lesser animals, the one's who live with humans but don't have a mortgage to pay for the change, still have the mental concept of the water hole. Even the human animal harkens to a deep memory of one. If he is wealthy enough, he may even have an artificial one in his back yard. He may call it a swimming pool, however. Few yuppies want to tell their potential rivals that they have a water hole in their back yard. The lesser status humans have to make do with public holes and fire hydrants; but the principle is there. We all depend on the old water hole in some form or another.

There is something to be said of clean water on demand. When I was young, it used to come from the kitchen and bathroom tap. I still get water from these sources, although it smells different. The older I get, the blonder I get. Someone has dumped chlorine and God only knows what else in my water hole. It still beats hacking my way through the reeds to the old water hole, hoping that a lion or leopard isn't looking; and kneeling in the mud for a swig of swill that was recently churned up by a herd of cape buffalos. Yes sir! Even that smelly, medicinal urban tap water is a high point of civilization.

Pet owners around the country instinctively establish the pet watering hole, usually in the kitchen and with some concern for decor. The water dish must match the curtains or what's a heaven for. If the pet is a slob, such as a beagle hound, a color coordinated place mat or rug complements the water hole. To simplify matters, the food dish stands promisingly near by. In my households, my mother's and mine, the food dish was kept filled with pet delights.

In that we usually had dogs as well as cats, what was in it really didn't matter. The first one there would scarf it all down in hopes that there would be none left for whoever happened to come after. Pets are very human in this regard. The dogs would eat the cat food and vice versus. It mattered not. These were just civilized frills on the old water hole. Getting snacks out of a dish is a heck of a sight easier than having to try to eat a full grown cape buffalo down at the old water hole; especially when he objected strenuously.

To pets, more than the concept of the water hole exists in their human habitat. Unburdened by the restrictions of language and propriety of conduct, to creatures who habituate a world less than a third of our normal human height, there exists a near perfect spring of clear, cool water. It is constantly there and easily accessible. To dogs, it is just chest high. To the agile cats, it is just a short jump up. It is the marvel of modern technology, the high point of civilization itself. For them, it is the reconstruction of their primordial habitat. It is the household toilet.

Every pet I ever had gravitated toward the old bathroom watering hole. At first, it gagged my prim and proper wife. Toilet Tonsils was her nickname for the uncouth imbiber. When our entire menagerie was so called, it became an endearment for them all. The toilet became a convenient spa to quench a thirst. Even if it were not up to the accustomed level of purity, it was still better than that swill a herd of Cape buffalo would stir up. The soggy paper would get caught in one's teeth, however. Fortunately, it was clean and cool most of the time.

In general, dogs seem to be a man's pet; whereas cats seem to be a woman's pet. While animal lovers have pondered this observed relationship, they have never hypothesized an adequate explanation for this phenomenon. I suggest that the explanation has to do with the accessibility of the watering hole. Consider this: dogs have no difficulty in accessing the refreshing contents of the toilet. They prefer that the wooden or plastic thingie that goes around the hole be up and out of the way. If it is down, the hole diameter is restricted. They bump their snoots on it on the way in and their heads on it on the way out. If they slobber all over it in a dog's manner, the mistress of the house screams bloody murder. Yes, the seat down is a nuisance. Seats are always up in a man's home; ergo: dogs prefer men.

Cats, on the other hand, are shorter than the run of the mill dogs. The edge of the water hole is slightly too high for ease of access. They have to balance their body on the wood or plastic thingie. If it is up, the surface is both very small and very slippery. What is more, it is very cold on the feet. Cats, being the hedonists that they are, find the seat up condition genuinely uncatly. When it is down, they have an adequate comfortably large and warm surface from which to fastidiously partake of the water. The seat is always down in a woman's home; ergo: cats prefer the company of ladies.

People who live in the country may have a somewhat different approach to the principle of the water hole. With a pond in the front yard, a stream in the meadow and a water dish constantly on the back porch, we had little need to set up a color-coordinated spa in the kitchen. Our animals were allowed in the house only after dinner. The pussycat that my wife and I had in our first house, Gladys, was a diminutive creature. Throughout her life, we always thought of her as a kitten as if she was always going to grow up. She never did. Her children dwarfed her. Gladys, needless to say, had some difficulty in accessing the water hole when she was in the house. Even in the seat down position, she had a precarious time of stretching all fours over the hole and lowering her head into position to get a drink. It was a real chore for her.

One evening after dinner, we were relaxing and watching the evening news in the living room. The bathroom, or water hole room, was just off the living room. Old country homes that predate Mr. Crapper have to press any convenient space into service. Our beagle hound, our sawed off collie pup, and Gladys were in the house. The fact that I didn't see them was not unusual. After dinner, all three would scrounge around the kitchen in search of some unguarded tidbit that we may have left in jeopardy. The evening clean- up consisted of cleaning the dishes and securing all edibles in a dog and cat proof container. We did outsmart them most of the time. We knew that they had to check things out, even though they were fed their rations and were apportioned all edible leftovers from the meal. I guess when you live the limited life of a pet; some things take on undo importance.

Whatever we had must have required water. Our tranquil evening was interrupted with a horrendous scream and splashing around. I rushed to the bathroom to intervene in what sounded like a drowning. Sure enough, it was! Poor Gladys was going down for the third time in the toilet while both dogs were drinking their fill and avoiding her thrashings. Gladys couldn't get a foothold on the porcelain and the dogs were pushing her under. I had to play lifeguard and save the young damsel in distress.

My wife and I pieced together what must have transpired. All three must have wanted a drink at the same time. Pigs, pets and people always want the same thing at the same time. The seat was up, so Gladys must have stretched herself precariously in her accustomed water hole position. The dogs, inconsiderate slobs that they are, must have bulldozed their way in and pushed poor Gladys to the brink of catastrophe. Life is precarious around the water hole. She survived the indignity but continued to use the toilet regularly. All three were just responding to the ancient instinct of the old water hole.

David R. Torrence

The Grey Ghost

We too often forget that pussycats come from a large family of wild animals. Their relatives account for some of the most efficient wild killers on this planet. Pussycats come from a distinguished family of predators. Like people, they have a wide range of personality types. Some are friendly and gregarious. Some are isolationists and hermits. All are individuals.

My camp, sometimes called my summer home by my mother and the lodge by my wife, was an old farmhouse that had fallen into disuse by changing economics. It served well as a base of operations for hunting and fishing forays into the surrounding boonies. In addition to the deer, bear, squirrel and turkeys that lived around the house, there was quite a few wee beasties that managed to live in the house.

The attic was loaded with bats. Before I became aware of the beneficial qualities of bats and became a bat defender, at dusk during a period of poor hunting, my buddy and I would blast away with our shotguns at the elusive targets to our frustrated heart's content. Bats are the penultimate clay pigeons. With spotlights after dark, we played "Battle of Britain". The shafts of light would criss-cross the sky until one of the "Bloomin' Jerries" would suddenly appear in the beam. A volley of fire and a roar of explosions would simulate that epic event. To the British ack-ack gunner who had no family in harms way, it must have been a real gas.

Mice were in the kitchen. Mice were actually everywhere, but the kitchen was their happy hunting grounds. Continual chemical and booby trap warfare never seemed to change their marauding numbers. In these terms, they won the war. Their numbers and activities, while kept under control, were about the same when I sold the place as when I bought it.

We had transient beasties. Each spring, at least one family of red squirrels and chipmunks would manage to rear their brood in a kitchen drawer somewhere. They had the poor manners of sitting on a table or dresser and announcing their displeasure at our arrival in a grating, high pitched chatter at four-thirty in the morning. While cute, they did not ingratiate themselves to me after a long drive and little sleep.

A few snakes were around the foundations. They had the good manners to stay out of our furniture and off the floors. We even had rattlesnakes in the area, but I found them to be rather gentle creatures who were quite content to be left alone. They could be heard slithering up to the attic between the walls. I always had mixed feelings about the snakes. I didn't want them; but then I didn't want the bats either. Or rather, I should say my wife didn't want the bats. I was jolted out of many a good night's sleep with a scream in my ear when one made a navigational error and began his evening's flight around the bedroom. It always fell to me to dispatch the poor beggar while my wife cringed and screamed under the covers. Bats, like cats, have an image problem. Now that environmental science has found them beneficial, I wouldn't dream of hurting one of the little beggars. My present home even sports a spiffy bat house to make amends.

It was only natural that an efficient predator should have moved into this haven of wee beasties. An old house is a total hunting environment for an entrepreneur like a cat. For the several years that I owned the camp, there was such an entrepreneur. I called him the grey ghost.

Ghost was an apt name for him. He was seldom seen and could disappear in a flash as if your eyes were playing tricks. I can only assume that he was a he. Ghost had the broad shoulders and strong jaw of a tom. In the several years that he "haunted" the house, there were never kittens. If ghost had been a lady cat, there surely would have been little ghosts. Cats are not good role models for modest behavior.

He was such an elusive creature that even when my parents stayed at the camp for extended periods of time, a glimpse of the ghost was still a rare thing. Whether he lived under the house or had just included the house in his hunting territory will never be known. He was always around, however. We knew he was around by his marks in the snow or his dirty paw prints on the back porch. Even when we had our other dogs and cats as house guests, he never made himself known.

When we accidentally caught sight of him, like all cats, he froze in his tracks. I guess all cats think like cats. If it doesn't move, it can't be seen. We would give the universal call of friendship: "Here kitty, kitty!" Ghost would have none of that. As soon as he realized that we had seen him, he would slip off and disappear in the nearest cover. He was a loner and as wild as any critter in those mountains.

A couple of our cat hating hunting neighbors had put him on their "target of opportunity" list. At least for two seasons, traps were set. Not that cat fur was paying top dollar or that they wanted cat burgers. Like Big Foot or the Abominable Snowman, Ghost became the target of curiosity hunters. It is a tribute to cats in general and Ghost in particular that he eluded them. I might add that one of the trappers was darn good. Ghost was a darn-sight better.

We could hear him from time to time. He never made a vocal sound, but we could hear him hunting in the basement. A woodchuck, another beastie that lived in our house, had dislodged a stone from the foundation and had made a regular doorway for himself and Ghost. At about eleven in the night, a regular "bump" could be heard. We could never be sure, but we always assumed it was Ghost. After all, it was an old house, and it was expected to be haunted by ghosts. I'm sure that a scientific explanation of ghosts and "things that go bump in the night" would probably be pussycats.

We had the camp for nineteen years. Ghost had been seen for the greater part of that time. We got a glimpse of him just months before we sold it. Perhaps, given the life span of a cat, Ghost was sort of our cat. I wish I could have said "good bye."

Handicapped

Handicaps are impairments of normal functions. Some are serious; and some are just nuisances. Everyone has some form of handicap in some aspect of life. We label them handicaps when they exceed some generally accepted level of what is normal. When we encounter someone who is blind or has lost a limb, we can definitely identify and will find universal agreement that there is a handicap. Unless one is unusually callous, one can feel sorry. Unfortunately, the handicapped only want and need empathy; not sympathy. A child that has a short attention span has a handicap, but most of society would not recognize nor sympathize with his plight. More than likely, he would be punished physically and socially for exhibiting the symptoms of his handicap. We have been walking in fashion footwear for so long in this country that we have forgotten what it is like to walk a mile in another's moccasins.

What I have difficulty in both sympathizing and empathizing with are those who choose to be handicapped. My heart does not go out to the individual who bemoans his or her lot in life because he or she is addicted to drugs or alcohol. I can't generate much feeling and concern for the girl who gets pregnant because she wants to be the queen bee of the local motorcycle gang. If normal, healthy individuals choose to become abnormal and unhealthy, is it my personal social and economic responsibility to rehabilitate those individuals just because they suddenly changed their minds or couldn't handle what they thought they wanted? It makes me angry when I see city councilmen complain vehemently that a school department wants a supplemental $11,000 to build wheelchair ramps; and then jump on a patronizing bandwagon and vote $75,000 for the expansion of the Drug Rehabilitation Program. Forgive my philosophizing but I personally have never recognized stupidity as a handicap. I must be callous. Am I handicapped? In the final analysis, the true measure of a society is how well it cares for its handicapped and aged.

The animal world has a way, albeit inhuman, of reducing the numbers of handicapped in their ranks. Animal mothers kill their malformed infants. I have observed this trait in dogs, pigs and pussycats. There are few natural handicaps among animals. Every now and then, however, one is encountered. It becomes somewhat of an oddity, and must rely on the Christian generosity of the human community for its survival.

63

One example of this occurred during my teen years. It seems that a cross-eyed kitten showed up in the community of my high school sweetheart. It was a pathetic creature; but cute as a button. The cross eyes added to its cuteness. From its actions, it was clear that its vision was horribly distorted. Nothing was where it appeared. It ran into things. If you gave it a tidbit, it missed mouthing the target by inches. We would have to put the food into its mouth; and it would be surprised because it didn't see it coming, at least from that direction. Getting a drink of water was a real chore. It began by poking its nose in the earth inches before the dish; then poking its little face closer and closer until by feel, it found it. Usually, it got a snoot full before the appropriate distance was felt.

Fortunately for the pussy, it was discovered by high school sophomores whose curriculum demanded their introduction to biology. It spent the rest of its life as the pampered guest of the local high school biology department. All it had to do for its survival was to be one of the department's living specimens. Unlike its caged or pickled counterparts, it had the run of the school and the concern of several thousand budding young scientists and their capable faculty.

Growing up, I did observe a number of cats, mostly streetwise toms that had lost limbs or eyes. Three legged or one-eyed cats were quite common in alleycatdom of the inner city. It's a tough life under the best of conditions. Trying to evade a dog, three kids and a slingshot is not conducive to careful crossing of busy intersections. If you're a vagabond and an orphan, there is no free community veterinarian clinic to which you can crawl. You heal or die in the cluttered back yard of some mom and pop store front business where there is sufficient respite to suffer. Those that did survive, like their human counterparts, did what they had to do; that is, do without. Life goes on. They functioned nearly as well as their non-handicapped competitors. Indeed, in some cases even better. By using their mind, they more than compensated.

Like so many of my cat guests, I "acquired" a handicapped pussycat because I had "a place in the country". I became a soft touch to anyone who wanted a divorce from his pet. This alienation of affection took place, as it does between humans, because of changing social and economic conditions: moving to another apartment, changing jobs, moving out of town, etc. Suburbanites know that the country is the better place to take unwanted animals. There is always room in the barn for another reject. I was on my way to my "camp" for a vacation when a faculty member who was changing his family status "conned" me into taking his apartment-reared pussycat along. It was quite a coup on his part because it was six hundred miles away.

I was introduced to "JD", short for John Dennis, who, frightened and wary, disappeared under my pickup truck's seat for the twelve plus hours it took to drive to my camp. He wouldn't even come out to relieve himself. I must say that I was a little concerned and miffed that he was probably taking care of his gastrointestinal needs in my truck. I waited for the telltale odor that would have released my fury that had been building since the realization that I had been conned into taking along a recalcitrant, unwanted passenger. The last thing I wanted was a cat.

Several times during the trip I diligently looked for him in the small confines of the pickup cab. I couldn't even find a pair of eyes peeking back at me. We were pretty sure that he hadn't jumped out somewhere along the interstate. The windows were closed or were guarded. In that I was in the tobacco-chewing period of my life, it was doubtful that he could have slipped out unnoticed. One does not lose track of an open window with a mouth full of tobacco juice. When we arrived, we managed to extricate a frightened and confused JD from the truck. How he managed the twelve hours without an "accident" I'll never know. I certainly couldn't do it; but then JD didn't drink coffee.

JD was a pretty cat. He was an all white, shorthaired cat with one eye as blue as the Chesapeake Bay in the days of my youth and the other eye as green as the Chesapeake Bay in the days of my "now". He looked different. He was different. He was handicapped. What my fellow faculty member didn't tell me was that he was as deaf as a doorknob. No wonder he didn't respond when I called to him, he couldn't hear me. This was a natural handicap that we had to learn to overcome.

He had two more handicaps that were induced. One, he was altered. This is always considered a good thing in the pet world. It is an impairment of a natural function, however, so it is a form of handicap. I wonder what the pets would say if they were consulted in this matter. Two, he had been declawed. His paws were as soft as the proverbial baby's bottom. This is also considered a plus in petdom. I could never feel comfortable with this induced handicap. I personally wouldn't do this to a cat. No creature should be denied their inalienable right of self-defense. Many, I'm sure, will take offense at my position, but I'm a creature of my past.

My early experience of watching cats having to fight for existence either with dogs, people or other cats has left me with a deep-seated conviction that pussycats need their claws. Even if they lost twenty five percent of them through accident, they still have a reasonably effective weapon. Most pussycats' world is the world of the sleazy bar and pool parlor, not the fenced and patrolled compound. Even the cat of the drawing room and compound will eventually slip out and go slumming. Life, liberty and the pursuit of food and sex in either order are their inalienable rights. This requires some self-defense on their part.

Over the years, I have willingly paid a price for my position. A whole parade of pussycats has left their marks on my inexpensive furniture. Starting in my mother's house, I have grown up with the idea that the first eighteen inches of all furnishings in the house should look as though it was low tide in an acid pool. The lower extremities of a cat's household will usually look like it is pulling away from the upper. Long striations in the wood and stalactites hanging from the stuffed furnishings give one a sense of dynamics. How many people can have a sense of change without adding to or deleting from the decor? I would holler at them; but they just waited until I wasn't there and then surprised me with the rearrangement of the basic design.

JD went through the motions of scratching with his claws. It was as pathetic as a eunuch whistling at a pretty girl. There was no substance in the act. I couldn't even enjoy hollering at him; although the first time or two it did cause a knee jerk response on my wife's part. Poor JD was never to know the thrill of a pulled fiber or the thrill of making a perfectly normal one hundred thirty pound human go ballistic. For pussycats, I'm sure there is a perverted sense of accomplishment in that.

JD's world had been an apartment. I later learned that he had never been outside. At the camp, he was injected into a different world. It was a world of motion, if not of sound. Every movement in the grass and bushes became an adventure. He took to outdoor- living with zest. If it moved, it was investigated. He would even make an attempt at climbing trees. He would run full tilt at a tree and transform his forward momentum upward. At times, he could run up a good five feet.

We were concerned that he couldn't hear something that should be heard. Nothing wild would bother him. Hunters and their dogs needed to be seen to be avoided; but we were torn between his love of the outdoors and our sense of protectiveness. I put myself in his place and decided upon the outdoors. Heck! What's the point of living if you're not living?

I remember well an experience with JD and his deafness. We spent a Christmas at the camp one year and erected a small Christmas tree on top of the television. When one sense is impaired, another takes on increased importance. In his world of silence, motion took on new meaning. A column of air was causing a tiny piece of tinsel at the top of the tree to shimmer. This fascinated JD. He would stare at it as if hypnotized for hours. Each day he would devote a goodly portion of his time to watch the top of the tree. In his absence, I would place myself in his position and watch. It was the slightest movement; but would cause a continual reflection of all the colors of the spectrum in never ending motion.

Then one evening, after a long vigil, he must have decided that he wanted it. He pounced upon the tree, shredded it and casually walked away. I thought that he may have had a fourth handicap: insanity. Cats are probably insane by human standards. But then, we are probably insane by theirs, and they are closer to nature. Are we insane by nature's standards?

The ultimate test of JD's handicap came when our neighbor came to his camp one weekend. He brought his entire family, inclusive of his pet German shepherd: Sheba. Her name should have been Brunhilda. She was a giant of a dog and twice as wild. She was controllable only at the end of a strained chain and under the threat of a big stick. Needless to say, Sheba saw a white cat playing around our house, so off she went. We saw the impending doom. We screamed for the cat out of sheer habit, but JD was involved in something else in his silent world. Sheba was bounding down upon him. We were too far off to even attempt intervention. It must have been vibrations in the ground or something, but JD turned suddenly just in time to see this monstrosity, seemingly snorting fire, bearing down on him.

Handicapped people are forced by circumstances to make do in spite of their handicap. If ever there was a time for adaptation, this was it. Claws or no claws, this was no time to feel sorry for one's self. JD took off cat like and went straight up a twenty-foot locust tree. The dog made a lot of noise, but JD was safely on a high limb. Only his tail, now three times wider than normal, showed his emotional involvement. He made it down on his own some time later when the coast was clear.

We all learned something that day. We learned that we didn't have to be so concerned about JD. He was quite capable of taking care of himself. JD learned that he could really climb trees. From then on, it was common to find JD some ten feet up in the branches of a tree chasing an illusive bird or just having the fun of doing something normal.

Another "acquired" guest was my little brother's cat: Ajax. Ajax was so named because at the time, Ajax Cleanser was running television ads that showed a white tornado running amuck inside a house. As a kitten in my mother's house, a white ball of fur ran through the house in similar fashion prompting the Madison Avenue programmed response of "there goes the white tornado"; ergo: Ajax.

He was a short haired, all white animal that somehow managed to stay sleek and slim in a household that sincerely believed that the best way to a cat's heart is through its stomach. Ajax beat the odds on corpulence but not in inner city navigation. He was run over by a car and suffered permanent injuries; losing control of his bladder and bowels. This is not a condition that is conducive to suburban living. The only visible sign of his injury was that be had no control of his tail. It just hung lifeless from his haunches. Showing no sign of immediate pain, he avoided the usual one-way trip to the vet. My brother, no doubt, was not up to the emotional strain. Euthanasia is not for the faint-hearted.

On better days, Ajax managed to move his impaired carcass with reasonable effectiveness. His toilet habits left something to be desired.

Ajax was no longer socially acceptable to suburban human culture. Handicapped people are often relegated to social Coventry.

As I was living in the country where social standards are more lax, Ajax was placed in my care; or my lack of care as the case may have been. It was a time when I was overrun with both excess dogs and cats. Perhaps it was for the best. Ajax was accepted as just one of the multitude. He managed to eke out a reasonably normal life. He "did his thing" as best he could until he died of other causes. The handicapped are just normal cats and people with impairment. Just give them a chance.

Happiness Is . . .

If you took a poll of the human population and asked them what they want most, the single most mentioned attainment would be "to be happy". True, what makes people happy may vary rather dramatically; but the end product is universal. We Americans even go so far as to place it among the lofty goals of our political existence. The pursuit of happiness is right up there with life and liberty in our Declaration of Independence and all subsequent legal documents. Happiness is good. Few would argue the point.

It is either our human incapacity to understand or our incredible species' ego that assumes the so-called "lower animals" don't have much the same goals in life. After a lifetime of observing my fellow mortal lower animals, I'm convinced that they too cherish life, liberty, and the pursuit of happiness. What is most reassuring is the fact that our lower animal brothers and sisters don't have to create elaborate institutions to guarantee these social goods to their fellow beings of the same species. It is taken for granted; a sort of Secular Animist philosophy.

Whole generations of lower animals have not had to sacrifice their freedom and jeopardize their lives and limbs to attain these social goods. While a young tom may be chased away from a willing lady or a tasty morsel by a dominant tom, only his pride and possibly his carcass are hurt, and that can be remedied by timely retreat. Pure "Aryan" Siamese cats have never launched a holocaust to exterminate their Persian brothers and sisters nor have they held their fellow Manx in subordinate bondage. It seems that the lower animals could care less about breeding.

True, the law of life is in operation among the various species. A cat will deny life, liberty and the pursuit of happiness to a passing mouse when he or she is hungry; but for the most part, the mouse is left alone to live out his existence until such time as the accepted and unchanging law of life is enforced. Usually, it is swift and merciful. The mouse is not herded into a concentration camp, managed by bureaucratic captors for some known and terrifying end. We all have to end in the end. Better to succumb to the law of life than to the operational orders of a military decision. Fortunately for the higher animal, few lower creatures make war. To my mind, only the ant is a fellow warrior and they only on a limited basis. Why do we persist in calling animals "lower" forms?

It doesn't take a gargantuan amount of the planet's resources to make a pussycat happy. A piece of silk in the sunshine, a stroking of the fur, nearly anything in motion or a chunk of liver constitutes pussycat happiness. There is no question in my mind that these menial attainments do create happiness.

One item that seems to create instant happiness in the feline world is catnip. Its effects, I can only surmise, are similar to alcohol or marijuana. He shows all the symptoms of getting a real "buzz" on. In that few cats drive automobiles or fly airplanes, it seems like an innocuous enough substance. It is difficult to determine whether it is use or abuse. Either way, Bob, my present feline child, is mildly addicted to his bag of catnip.

Several months ago, I bought several ounces of fresh catnip from a nearby herb farm. Not knowing how to present this present to Bob, I put a little loose catnip on his feed dish. Other than a few sniffs and a sneeze, he seemed rather unconcerned. Actually, he seemed rather disappointed. A hefty snack of canned Pussycat Glop would have been better received. A cat does have expectation, and that stuff had all the appeal of a cup of dried tea leaves. Icht!

A friend of the family who has an artistic flair and a sewing machine put the catnip in a little cloth bag complete with his name painstakingly embossed on each side; a sort of catnip bean bag. If not a consumable commodity, why not a toy? . . . sparkling white, name-embossed new toy?

When we presented it to Bob, he didn't seem to be much interested in that either. True, he sniffed it with more inquisitiveness. He did bat it, but only once. After all, if it didn't roll, what good was it? I was sorely disappointed. My gift was not well received. It was like buying my conservative father-in-law a pair of Reboks. He hasn't worn anything but wingtips since the late 40's. The customary "thank you" was more a questioning of my intelligence rather than an expression of gratitude. Pussycats are not creatures of false emotion.

It was some time later that we discovered that Bob had indeed developed an interest in his new toy. He must have been sandbagging us, or catnip bagging us as the case may be. He seemed to like it. He licked it. He rubbed his face in it. He held it between his paws and rubbed and licked. He hugged it and rolled on the floor with it. Actually, he made a fool of himself with it, much to our amusement. He seemed to reach for something in that bag that was providing him with obvious pleasure. It reminded us of the seeming sensual satisfaction that babies derive from their pacifiers. This was a catnip "binky".

The darn stuff really works! I have never researched the natural agents of catnip or its chemical effects. It seems to have the same effect as alcohol or marijuana. In either case, Bob appears to get a real "buzz" on. Euphoria? Hallucination? Peace? I wonder. Whatever it is, it doesn't seem to have any debilitating effects. He can walk away from his disgustingly sensuous romps with his binky without any sign of incapacitation or impairment. Nor has it become a habitual fixation replacing any of his other activities. He still eats well, sleeps well, is found occasionally in unusual places such as the breadbasket on the top of the refrigerator, and terrorizes the local population of starlings and neighborhood dogs.

His interest is only occasional. About once a day, he will crawl under the microwave stand and engage in an orgy of self-gratification with his binky. The bag has been relegated to beneath the microwave for the sake of propriety. The nice white bag has become a rather disgusting shade of brownish amber from weeks of licking and slobbering, not to mention the innumerable face rubbings. His embossed name has long since disappeared. The bag has become too obscene for polite company. My non-pet owning friends do not understand the level of cleanliness that our non-human children are apt to find acceptable.

At times, only his lower body can be seen rolling and gyrating in obvious pleasure. Often, he will lay on his back hugging his binky, exposing his unmentionables in a most obscene manner. When he pulls his binky out from under the stand, he appears to wrestle with it. He loves it. After all, happiness is a catnip binky!

Hedonists All

The dictionary defines hedonism as: The doctrine that pleasure is the sole or chief good in life and that moral duty is fulfilled in the gratification of pleasure seeking instincts and dispositions. The great thinkers of the ancient world who formulated this philosophy must have used their rational powers and made observations from the natural world to arrive at this rather delightful but impractical goal. No doubt, in the far distant past, a great thinker must have been watching his pussycat and said to himself: "He knows how to live!" Eat, drink, and be merry, for tomorrow you may die. If any creature on this planet has this as its credo, it is the pussycat. I can think of no other animal that exemplifies hedonistic tradition more fully. For those of us who have cats, we can testify to the fact that they are creatures that seek pleasure and avoid pain. This is one of their endearing charms.

Unlike the self indulgent human who appears to revel in his pleasure only in front of or at the expense of an audience, the self-indulgent pussycat appears to exude pleasure totally in his solitude. Like Hindu mystics, they seem to internalize their world when in a state of orgasmic relaxation. How does science explain the "purr"? I'm sure a medical analysis would say something like: "it is the forced passage of air across the 'thoraxial thingamagadget' when in the relaxed state". Big deal! How many other of God's creatures even have a "thoraxial thingamagadget" much less find the time to lay around exercising it. Indeed, the pussycat has been endowed with a marvelous dimension. The "purr" may be the ultimate alternative to sex. If humans had the capacity to "purr" in the purist sense, it would probably be a sinful act. "Bless me father for I have sinned. Two night's ago I purred."

"Were you alone, my son"?

"Yes father, I purred all alone".

"Remember son, your body is the temple of the Holy Ghost. You should not abuse or debase your body. Say ten Our Fathers and ten Hail Marys and purr no more".

Sinful or not, I wish I had the capability to purr. It looks like it would be great!

Another of their charms is the fact that they are sensualists. No creature is as sensual or sensualistic as are pussycats. They revel in sensuality. They love to rub and be rubbed, stroked, held, scratched, or whatever. True, dogs love to be petted, but cats seem to respond to the act in itself; not the meaning behind the act. Like the human female, they are creatures that live on their nerve endings. It is no wonder that women are often called catlike. They seem to share sensuality. But, it is important to note that the woman is said to be catlike and not the cat to be women-like. In sensuality, the pussycat is supreme.

When it is cold, I have seen my cats find a spot of sun the size of a fifty-cent piece and curl up into it. If a piece of silk or soft fabric is casually thrown on the bed, it becomes an instant pillow for one of my sensualistic pussycats. My wife doesn't realize that her underwear turns everyone in the house on although for different reasons.

Hedonism can and does get pussycats into trouble at times. They, being both practical and sensualistic, manage to survive even in the worst of conditions. I know of and have heard of several instances where pussycats, seeking the last vestige of warmth during a cold night, have sought comfort by curling up for a good night's snooze on the still warm engine block of a car. In the morning, without their first cup of coffee or its cat equivalent and in a bleary eyed stupor, they are chopped to pieces by the fan blade. It is a rather ghastly way to meet the Great Pussy in the Elysian catnip fields in the sky. A friend of mine has had the unfortunate luck to chop up not only his wife's pet cat, but their two replacements. He says he shudders every time he puts a key into the ignition.

They even appear to derive sensual pleasure from the act of keeping clean. My dogs seem to have reveled in their filth. A well rubbed-in dead fish or snake is worn by a dog as a beauty

79

mark.   Cats, on the other hand, are unscrupulously clean.   A snack can evoke a complete bath from head to toe. Cleaning and preening are the cat equivalent to the cigarette after. If they can't reach a spot with the tongue, they lick their paws and scrub. They put so much into the act that I detect some ulterior, sensualistic motive. I love a hot shower; but not after every meal.

My dogs didn't like a hot shower anytime. The only time they ever licked their fur was to extract the last bit of grease or gravy that might have stuck to them during one of their less than fastidious feedings.   Perhaps "feedings" is too polite a word.   For dogs, it would be better described as a food orgy. Only my pigs showed less gentility when it came to eating. Cats, on the other hand, are quite fastidious; and finicky. Morris, the late, great "Duke" of catdom, attested to this fact.

Another of a pussycat's endearing quirks is that of kneading.   People and pussycats come from a long line of mammals; those highly specialized creatures that produce milk and suckle their young. While the obvious advantage of providing nutrition to the young is central to this unique characteristic, scientists have discovered a whole set of psychological side effects that are essential to good mental health. To put it bluntly, sucking on a ninny is good for you.   As a species, our seemingly absurd obsession with mammary glands is probably rooted in this psychological relationship.   They are the last external umbilical cord between peace and contentment and the cold, cruel world. Subliminal fond memories are attached.

As with any piece of equipment in this physical world, you have to know how to get the thing to work. Nature, in its questionable wisdom, did not put spigots on them. It is not enough just to suck on them. Boobs are, in fact, highly complicated chemical factories. Milk is not stored; it is produced on demand at the end of an assembly line that requires the throwing of the proper switches and the coaxing of the gears. The tactile stimulation of an infant's tongue and the gentle, rhythmic throb is equivalent to the foreman's gentle patting and timely nudges on the gauges.

Pussycats, creation's arch hedonists, have developed an instinctual, rhythmic action to produce the mammary response. To the human observer, it is analogous to kneading bread. To watch kittens at the feeding trough is like watching at the gym. Each station is massaged vigorously as if each kitten was on an exercycle. Kneading has become so internalized that any pleasurable experience will trigger the kneading response in adults; in some, more than others. Bob, my present white step kitten, will break into kneading every time I scratch his head. If he stands on my rather generous stomach, he breaks into purring and kneading. The expression on his face is one of utter contentment. Oh, to return to the secure, comfortable feelings of our respective infancy!

David R. Torrence

As the kittens become cats, the kneading becomes a little more pronounced. With increased strength, the rhythmic action becomes more like being pushed in a crowd. What is worse, those gentle, soft paws of kittens develop rather effective claws. With each shove, those sharp needles protrude beyond the protective sheathe of the paw and hang up in the warp and woof of twenty dollar shirts. The midsection of all my shirts have telltale Irish Pennants that my litany of pussycat stepchildren have left me as a legacy of contentment. On tee shirts or bare skin, kneading is downright painful; in the wrong spot, downright dangerous.

But, as mammals, we are empathetic creatures. The next best thing to receiving pleasure is to give pleasure. There is some satisfaction in the giving. Pussycats have capitalized on this phenomenon to the fullest. If you want to see the effect of giving pleasure and contentment, get a pussycat for a pet. So what if your shirts or dresses look a little seedy. Everyone needs a little kneading.

Perhaps those who don't like pussycats dislike them for their pagan ways. To the ultra-conservative Christian, their images on Egyptian tombs prove their pagan associations. Always unjustly associated with witches, warlocks, and other demonic practices, the one very unchristian characteristic is their observably religious adherence to the pagan practice of hedonism. Cats have been the "mediums" for witch craft since medieval times. Watching pussycats in the sun with a sinful grin on his face makes one believe that maybe they have the truth, the light, and the way. It works for them.

He Who Fights and ...

When in a hurry, the speed of the fornication process of pussycats lies somewhere between the snap of a mousetrap and lightning. I sometimes wonder if there is any orgasmic impetus to their endeavor. The only visible sign of enjoyment appears to be in their foreplay; and this is always when they are by themselves. The ladies roll and gesture; the gentlemen strut and posture. In actual practice, the females act as like victims of Dracula; and males more like riveting guns.

The foreplay episode invariably draws prospective suitors from great distances. Once arrived, they are under pressure to justify their presence to their competitors in combat. I often think that this behavior is exactly what our European progenitors engaged in during the medieval times. For the hand, or whatever, of your lady, you had to first fight a dual; not to the death, but for supremacy. This was conducted according to rules. You made your entry rattling and clanging in your armor. This was so they could hear you. You wore bright colored shields, banners and flags. This, so they could see you. You then had to vanquish each of your foes by trying to knock him off his horse. This required you to charge at full tilt and bash him with a reinforced clothes prop while he returned the courtesy. The lady went off with the victor, whoever he might be. Quite frankly, after a round of foreplay such as this, a romp in bed would have been the last thing I would want. Heck, let her complain to her father that I wasn't interested. Between bruises, broken ribs and stiff muscles, the sex act seemed unimportant. It must be so with cats.

One of the many part time jobs I had as a youth to pay for school and to pursue the ladies was a job delivering liquor; a case of beer to this house, three fifths to that, and so on. Several evenings a week and all day Saturday was my schedule for several years. Jobs such as this took me into many households. Politicians should only be recruited from the ranks of delivery route men. It gives one a unique perspective of humanity. It also provides a panoply of experiences that one could never amass in other fields.

One evening as I stopped the store's station wagon under a city lamp post to double check an address, I became aware of an incredible noise emanating from my immediate vicinity. On inspection, I discovered that I had parked in a grandstand seat for a pussycat joust. Not less than a dozen toms formed an undulating circle around a female who was obviously in heat. Under the glow of the streetlight, she rolled and gestured in an exotic and lurid display.

The toms were sizing up their competition. The noise was a cacophony of guttural growls and raucous squeals that would drown out the noise of an army of squeaking bulldozers. Each combatant had to yell his litany of insults to all who would listen. I became entranced as one becomes enthralled in the preliminaries before the main fight. Tension was in the air.

The lady continued her sensual displays as if she was totally uninterested as to who crossed no man's land for her favors. In point of fact, she didn't. La donna mobile' and all that. The noise continued for some time.

All at once, on no apparent cue, all of the suitors suddenly rushed into clawing, slashing, squalling combat. It was a sight that could best be described as a cartoon caricature. There was a massive ball of fur in furious motion, blurred by the inability of the eye to focus upon individuals. Individual heads, tails, and patches of fur were in focus only for short periods of time as the great free for all pulsated in deadly earnest.

The war continued for a surprisingly long time. No individual seemed to emerge the winner. Suddenly, a typical alley tiger popped out of the furry blur; his absence seemingly unobserved. In a microsecond, he ran over to the gyrating lady, bit her neck, performed his rivet gun antics and jumped back into the fray. The free for all continued unabated. I was in a state of humorous disbelief.

I have no recollection of the final outcome. I only remember the enterprising tom who obviously was goal oriented. He certainly exercised good judgment. Was he prompted by the thought that he was losing the fight; if so, what great forethought. He could be driven off, but only with the self-satisfaction that "he got his". Why did he return to the fight? Was it that much fun? I'll never forget that feline opportunist. He taught me about life. He, who keeps his eye on the prize, lives to fight another day . . . or something like that.

Lead Foot

The agility and stealth of cats has been both admired and feared throughout the centuries. To say that an athlete moves like a cat is to pay him or her the highest compliment. Catlike is synonymous with grace, poise, athletic prowess and, to a great degree, quietness. "As quiet as a cat" is as prevalent a cliché' as "quiet as a mouse". The person who coined the latter phrase must have had a cat.

People who hate cats justify their irrational malevolence with such statements as: "they're sneaky" or "they're creepy". What they are saying is that they are catlike. To this, I can offer no defense. You either take them as God made them or create some human or demonic rationale to sustain your bigotry. Cat haters probably also hate blacks, honkies, Spics, Gooks, Catholics, Protestants, Jews, male chauvinists, women, and

. . . , my apologies if I left anyone out. Irrationality knows no bounds.

For those of us who have been around cats, we realize that there are cats and there are klutzes. While the cat person purist will vehemently dispute this slander, some cats are not as catlike as others. I have run into a few that exhibit all the clumsiness and cloddish moves of grade B, burlesque slapstick. Not many I will admit, but a few.

To watch cats' long stalk is to watch a ballet. On numerous occasions, I have enjoyed watching my cats stalk an unsuspecting bird or chipmunk. My gentle, butter wouldn't melt in their mouth, rag doll pussycats turn into precision killers. They assume the catlike crouch, muscles taught, short darting moves, eyes fixed on their quarry. This near perfect organic machine has one minor flaw. Nature somehow goofed; or has become inscrutable to say the least. In the thrill of the hunt, the cat's childlike enthusiasm is transmitted to the tip of their tail. While the main portion of the cat can be motionless and poised for the pounce, the tip of the tail is bouncing around like a snake charmer's cobra. It seems that nature provided this last minute "edge" for the prey. If they are truly wary, they could spot this movement as if pussycat was waving a flag. The success rate is pretty bad. Not because pussy didn't creep, belly to the ground for a low profile, not because he or she didn't move when the quarry wasn't looking, not because pussy lost his or her attention momentarily; it was because they were advertising their stalk as surely as if by a squad of over zealous pom-pom girls.

I'm sure the lethal lunge could catch the unwary. Young backyard robins and hand fed chipmunks are not nature's fittest for their species' survival. Man turns everything into pansies. I always yell before the fatal rush and warn the expected victims. The pussycats always look back at me with that tell tale gaze that says: "You dirty *&^%$". I'm always forgiven for the breach of hunter's etiquette, however. They always know that I reimburse them for their loss with some succulent can of Pussy Good cat food. There must be a bright side to induce a pussycat to partake of this civilization nonsense. After all, who wants to eat a scrawny worm fed robin or a nutty chipmunk? That's garbage compared to what's in those laboratory designed, taste test blended cans of whatever. Only God and the manufacturer know what comprises processed cat food; but it sure smells good, that is, of course, if "stench" is any indication of palatability.

Bob White, my present cat child, is one of those creatures that is a generous blend of poise, grace and klutzism. At one moment, he can be a picture of nature at its best. At another, he is comedy at its worst. I've seen him slink across twenty yards of open terrain and nearly pounce on a mocking bird. He'll never do that again! Mocking birds hold grudges.

I've seen Bob leap several times his height atop a polished dresser and slide completely off the opposite side, careening into pile of furry wreckage with complete loss of dignity. I'm sure my laughter is of greater pain than the fall.

It is not totally true that cats always land on their feet. True, they do most of the time. They do enough to convince the non-cat owning general public that landing on their feet is Newton's thirteenth law of motion. Bob and others have convinced me not to bet unduly large sums of money on this phenomenon. Bob, the great bug catcher, makes frantic leaps upon his bug sized prey and crashes on the first part of his body to intercept the earth; rarely his feet. Bob is a klutz!

Probably, the most uncatlike quality in Bob is his gait. While most cats walk with the grace of a ballerina, Bob clomps along like Charlie Chaplin. It causes a laugh or at least a smile in either my wife or me when we hear him walk through the house. There is no doubt where he is, even if we can't see him. He "thump-thumps" through the house as if he weighed fifty pounds. He is the antithesis of catlike behavior. At these times I've dubbed him: Lead foot.

David R. Torrence

Almost Life-like

Cats are beautiful animals. Whether lions, tigers, pumas or pussycats, they are magnificent to watch. Even people who hate cats have to admit that they are good looking creatures. They hate them for some other reason; usually, they describe some personality trait that they find abhorrent. Almost always, the trait is one that they themselves exhibit: cats are sneaky, cats are cruel, and cats kill rabbits. Cats are just too human like.

Because of their beauty, cats have been the subjects of art throughout the centuries and across cultures. During the 50's and early 60's, cats were the objects of statuary. Statues of cats in the sitting position began to be seen in many middle class households during this time. Some were surrealistic; carved out of exotic woods with jeweled eyes. Others were ceramic with smooth lines and exotic colors. Most were quite lifelike. The black cat in the ancient Egyptian stance was the most common.

One afternoon during the liquor delivery period of my life, I made a stop to a lovely furnished home. Inner city houses are individualized only from the inside. The outsides are all the same. This was obviously a well kept, well furnished home. I made the delivery and stood in the living room while the lady of the house went to get the appropriate funds. In her absence, my eyes scanned the room in admiration.

Atop the Danish modern bookcase at the foot of the stairs, barely a yard from me stood the most beautiful cat statue I had seen to date. It was magnificently carved; so lifelike. It was huge; what appeared to be nearly half again life size. It was black; nearly iridescent black. The tail curled around the feet in excellent execution. The eyes truly made the statue. How on earth did the artist capture that color and depth of the eyes? They appeared to nearly glow.

I admired that motionless statue for some time; what I thought was a full five minutes. I moved in for an even closer view. Yes, this was the best statue that I had ever seen. It went with the impeccable furnishings of the house. With my face a matter of inches from the statue, while admiring those penetrating eyes, one of them blinked. I jumped back startled.

The lady returned to the room and realized my intense involvement with her "statue". "Oh, that's 'Who's-a-what's-it'," the name never registered. "Isn't he a lovely cat. 'Who's-a-what's-it' blinked again. He was real. I felt like a fool; and me, the mighty hunter. After some cat talk and an exchange of money, I left the household forever.

With so many statues very lifelike, he was so statue-like. How he managed to remain totally motionless for so long is still a marvel. I still admire those cat statues; and will always remember the one that blinked at me.

Lily

Cats have a great number of attributes that recommend them to pet status. They are small, cuddly, soft, warm, affectionate, pretty, and so forth. The fact that they are America's number one pet choice comes as no surprise. They have a number of redeeming qualities that make them pleasant to have around. For one thing, they are mammals. They possess all the mammalian physical and psychological dimensions that we humans posses. We can more or less understand each other even without a common language. We can empathize with hunger and thirst, excitement, fear, the thrill of victory and the agony of defeat, and all that.

A second important quality is that they are trainable. They can be molded to live within the human context of life. For instance, they can be potty trained faster than any other pet I can think of with the possible exception of goldfish that have no choice in the matter. The inventor of kitty litter should be ranked among the greatest inventors of the modern era. Introduce a cat to your home, its food dish and the kitty litter box and you have instant pet.

I could enumerate all the splendid characteristics of pussycats for many pages, possibly volumes, and would still probably offend some cat person who would discover that I left out some real or imagined virtue. It wasn't until recently that they became the number one pet choice. There is a reason. Cats have their shortcomings as well as their attributes.

The saying goes: "Love is blind". For the animal world, this must be so. The sense of smell seems to be more important than the sense of sight when it comes to love in the afternoon. What if we humans had developed this sense in judging a prospective mate's attractiveness? Just imagine a group of young men sniffing the air and exclaiming: "Wow! Smell that chick!" Maybe we have lost a very exciting dimension. Pussycats haven't, however. The toms still have the ancient urge to announce their olfactory presence with a little squirt here and a little spray there. I'm sure it must be stimulating to the lady cats that must sniff and say: "Now here's a real stud!" To us desensitized humans, we say that it smells like cat urine. Why not; heck, it is! Let's call a spade a spade. This has never endeared cats to modern human habitation. Male cats seem to get their you-know-what's cut off at a significantly higher rate than do male dogs. The overriding negative point to having a cat as a pet is odor. True, this can be controlled; but it looms high in the minds of many.

Another point to their discredit is, as with any carnivore, their digestive process leaves something to be desired. The bacterial breakdown of protein does cause some negative olfactory sensation. Let's face it; cat stuff stinks! I'm using cat "stuff" in an effort to appease some more sensitive reader. For the realist, you know to what synonym I'm referring. In fact, it is normally used as a statement of the superlative. To say that someone is as mean as cat "stuff" is to say that he excels to the pinnacle of meanness. Cat crap is the measure from which to judge all other odors. This is why the kitty litter inventor deserves his recognition.

For some strange and perverted reason, the bodily waste, whether solid, liquid or gas, and from any orifice is of the utmost interest if not importance to us all. Children and old people are intensely interested in the solid waste; though for different reasons. Children, primarily, are enthralled to discover their control over the emissions of body gas either as a belch or, shall we say, "breaking wind". There is no polite way of phrasing the ever-popular "fart". Little boys derive great pleasure in both discussing and perpetrating the emission of body gas. As youngsters, my disgusting crew of pre-pubescent imps humorously described this capability as "dropping lilies". No description could be less appropriate.

Interest in this animal capability dissipates with age in an indirectly proportional manner to intelligence. The chronological and mental eight-year old appreciates the sound and odor of a good belch or flatus. I have observed gas emission contests among third graders and among red neck bar beer drinkers. In point of fact, I am only slightly ashamed to say, that, given enough alcohol and carbohydrates, I have participated in these events. The sophisticated adult human puts this natural phenomenon into the category of unrecognized events. There are some things in life we don't discuss; mostly through fear of coming to grips with our animal origins.

Every now and then, the phenomenon hits us without warning, most often in the nose, and we're suddenly thrust back to childhood memories. At such times, even the most dignified adult is reduced to a smile if not all out belly-laughter. The degree of humor is always directly proportional to the remoteness of the source. When you are involved, it is not funny. When "they" are involved, it is invariably hilarious. When your pussycat is involved, it is both funny and superlative. When a pussycat breaks wind, it takes first place in the odor contest. Whew!

Just the other day, my fuzzy white stepchild, Bob, came running down the stairs with his ears back as though he was being chased by something. My wife and I were busy looking for something when we were interrupted by his entry upon the scene. The search required us to look in the bedroom from whence Bob had made his hasty exit. Upon entering the room, we were overwhelmed with obvious cat odor. "Oh, he didn't!" my wife exclaimed; "Watch where you walk". There was no evading the situation, an "event" had transpired. We were taken back that

Bob would have gone to the potty in "his" room. He was so well trained.

Surely, something was amiss. We searched for the odoriferous ejecta; our noses being the direction finders. The odor hung heavy in the room but could not be pinpointed. It was just there . . . floating in space. In a little while, it dissipated. We were relieved that Bob had not resorted to the unmentionable practice of "having accidents". Cat accidents are minor disasters.

It was then that the humor of the situation hit us. We rolled in laughter. No wonder Bob had made such a hasty exit. He couldn't stand it any more than we could. Bob had dropped a lily.

Not So Endearing Young Charms

In an effort to be objective on the topic of pussycats, which I obviously am not, I feel compelled to enumerate on some of those characteristics that my cat hater friends find some sort of cynical pleasure in pointing out. I apologize to my cat people readers, but, alas, 'tis true; cats are not creatures of perfection. They have some characteristics that are less than endearing.

Some people are allergic to cats. My brother, Bill, is a good example. He actually likes cats.

What is worse, they like him. Given the opportunity, cats will be all over him; rubbing, purring, dragging their tails across his face, etc. They exhibit every outward sign of true affection. Maybe, of course, they know he is allergic and are going to go the extra mile to make him suffer. Cats are devious little devils at times.

And suffer he does. If he goes into a cat owner's house, the symptoms become apparent in a matter of minutes. His eyes turn red from his pupils to his cheeks. He begins to cough and sneeze as if on cue. I'm sure if he didn't get relief, he'd probably die. The tears run down his red cheeks as if someone just put a gouge down the complete length of his Mercedes Benze. Not that he has one, mind you. All his life he has admired them; so I thought this might be a good analogy.

As an adult, it pains me to see another human being in such distress. When I was his mean kid brother, I'd bring cats into the house just to watch him wheeze. Kids are devious little devils, too. Maybe we like cats because they remind us of our children and ourselves. I've never heard of anyone being allergic to dogs. What is the difference? I have known several other people who were or said they were allergic to cats. I'm sure there is a perfectly sound scientific explanation for the phenomena; but it doesn't seem to help the sufferer. Unless one is a devoutly dedicated masochist, I would not recommend a cat for a pet to someone with allergies. There truly is trouble in Paradise.

Another troublesome characteristic is hair. True, dogs have hair also. With the possible exceptions of the Mexican hairless dogs, tropical fish, and reptiles, most pets have hair or feathers that somehow manage to cling to clothing and furniture. While this is a universal problem across pets, cats seem to have the "clingiest" hair. It permeates the environment.

I attempt to look like a businessman. In true, "Dress for Success" style, I have garnished my wardrobe richly with high-authority suits. For my proletarian readers, a high authority suit is a dark suit, usually a navy blue with a faint vertical pin stripe. Rich woolens are better than synthetics. Decked out in my high authority suits, I feel like a cheap politician; but I look lofty. At least I did until my present feline stepchild moved in.

Bob, my present pussycat, is white. Bob likes me. He likes Purina cat food more, but I come in a close second. Early on, he has discovered that to get to number one, he has to rub the complete length of his body across the legs of number two. This has become a ritual. Not that this is restricted to feeding time, mind you. Hope springs eternal. Even chance encounters elicit the Purina petting syndrome. My high authority suits have become magnets for his hair. The first eighteen inches of my pants usually possesses three quarters as much hair as the original owner. No matter how much masking tape is expended on keeping my pants hair free, I always look seedy. White hair on a dark suit is not conducive to eliciting authority. The illusion is that I'm wearing fuzzy, faded bell-bottoms.

Cat hairs are not confined to high authority suits. They seem to show up everywhere. One of those places is in your mouth. How often while eating, I encounter that minuscule something that is obviously not edible. There is no graceful way to extricate the now slimy, food-encrusted follicle from your mouth. I try not to dominate the casual discussions of the dinner table; but inevitably, I'm the center of everyone's attention when I encounter the errant hair in the mouth. All eyes seem to attend my interruption of the topic at hand to remove the unwanted object. Perhaps the crowd forms spontaneously when they see the abbreviated masticatory gestures when one encounters a hair.

Even the eyes show the shift of emphasis from external to internal. You can spot the person who has a hair in the mouth. The chews become shallow and frequent. The eyes look down. A questioning scowl appears on the victim's face. All combine to telegraph his plight: "Hey! Everybody! I got a hair in my mouth!" The ultimate decision that is made as one pulls it spaghetti-like from the mouth is: Is it the cook's; the cat's, or his own? Ninety-nine times out of a hundred, it is the cat's. Pussycat fur has that unique property of being wafted aloft upon the balmy zephyr, right into your soup.

Another of their characteristics that my cat hating friends like to charge is that cats jump up on everything. It's true, I must confess. Some cat haters use the statement that they get up on the table; and "who wants to eat where some cat was sitting". Good point! . . . or butt if I may make the pun. It assumes that we live in a more or less sterile environment to start with.

Cats do get into trouble with their "get into everything" meanderings. My former neighbor had an incident wherein his insurance company named the cat the culprit. There was no other conclusion in that the cat was the only living, moving creature in the household at the time. It seems that my neighbors were going away for the weekend. They didn't want to leave their pet pussycat to wander the neighborhood without adult supervision. We humans never seem to realize that an adult cat is not equivalent to an adolescent human. My experience with adolescent humans is that anything on this planet is smarter, inclusive of germs. One can get over a cold in two weeks; whereas it takes years to get over adolescence.

My neighbor was a professional photographer. Among the many rooms of his house, he had a basement darkroom. As with most American matriarchal households, the male is relegated to the basement. All of his hunting and fishing gear, his tools, his camping equipment, all his valued out of doors gear was consigned to the deepest and darkest recesses of the house. Men should be kept in their place; right ladies?

For those readers who are unfamiliar with photo dark room procedures, one of the processes to get a photograph is to wash the chemicals from the photographic paper. The good ones are processed and given to admiring recipients. The bad ones usually never get beyond the darkroom sink. A photographer's darkroom sink is the equivalent of a writer's trashcan. The pussycat was left in the house all by herself; complete with a fresh kitty litter box, water, and a fair size mountain of dry cat food. What could go wrong?

As was pieced together by the insurance claims man, the pussycat went exploring in the darkroom. Somehow, she managed to turn the water on in the sink. Large handles on the taps are needed when working in the dark. The failures of the last photographic project quickly stopped up the drain; and, for an entire weekend, the water ran. It is amazing how a concrete lined hole in the ground can contain so much water. Needless to say, when they returned home, they had a basement full of water . . . really full. All of his cherished goodies were floating or submerged beneath the deluge. The cat, totally unconcerned, was found fast asleep on their bed. The old cliché: curiosity killed the cat wasn't applicable to my neighbor's situation; but curiosity played a part in his loss of all his cherished goodies. His pussycat didn't endear itself to him. Post insurance claim, the cat was thenceforth referred to as his "wife's" cat.

Even when they know that they're not to be atop something or other, they will get up. You come to know that they know better. They have a way of making a hasty exit before you catch them in the act. They inspect every surface inch of the household on a regular basis. Those telltale cat hairs appear in the most incredible places.

Just yesterday, I observed this deviant behavior. My wife was on the phone; my son had finished his breakfast and left the table. I was in the kitchen surveying in a lord of the manner fashion my confusing, noisy domain. Bob, my white haired, brazen stepchild and pussycat, jumped upon the dining room table. He maneuvered with the grace of a ballet dancer amid the aftermath of the meal; sniffing as he went for gustatory opportunities. My wife flailed the air as if to drive him off. Bob knew he was not allowed on the table. He also knew that the telephone cord was too short to allow her anywhere near him. He also knew human nature. He knew that she would not leave the end of the cord, even for a second, to drive him off. She seemed to dangle and gyrate on the end of the telephone cord as if it were a high voltage power line. Bob casually strolled over to my son's place and found his discarded milk.

Most people believe that animals are incapable of problem solving. If the preceding events haven't convinced you, perhaps these subsequent events will. The milk was in a cup. Bob couldn't get his fat head in the cup; so he had to improvise. Aesop's story of the crane and the fox was enacted before my eyes. Bob casually stuck the end of his paw in the wanted milk until it was saturated. He then licked his paw. He repeated this several times until my wildly gyrating wife turned to me to intervene. I had no sooner made two steps across the floor than Bob made a hasty exit. He knew that I was not attached to the end of a telephone cord. If this isn't problem solving then I would like to hear a reasonable explanation.

Another of the more unpleasant characteristics of pussycats is attributed to the male of the species. Harkening to the primordial territorial urge of their progenitors, the tom pussycat must put his seal of approval and ownership on those things he deems his. Unfortunately, what is his is what you thought was yours. What is more, his idea of proper identification is not your idea of appropriate identification. Humans report property to the insurance company. Pussycats wee-wee on it. "Spraying", the more polite way of saying "pissing upon", is one of those not so endearing young charms of pussycats; not that it often isn't an appropriate evaluation of the object in question, but it is just not done in polite human society.

Nor is the act of wee-weeing on things in and of itself particularly bad; if that was all there was to it. Unfortunately, the process involves urine. In that, the tom's aroma excels all except the renowned skunk. Actually, weasels, mink, etc. are worse; but few humans come in contact with these rather unusual creatures. Even the uninitiated can detect a house of unrestrained toms. Unaltered toms are creatures of the rural habitat. Urban male cats are either altered pets or wild vagabonds. For those who have a hyper developed olfactory sense, tomcats are not the pets of choice.

One little known problem with pussycats is a condition called toxoplasmosis. I never heard of it before the age of thirty. My wife and I discovered after some ten or so reckless and irresponsible years that children do not come easy to some people. Human pregnancy obeys Murphy's Laws. An unmarried, teenybopper dilettante is often more at risk than a family seeking married couple. We sought unsuccessfully for years. On several occasions, a delayed period brought forth hope; but this always ended in a few anxious days.

In the tenth year, a ray of hope occurred. The days became weeks. Hopes ran high. The doctor confirmed, with the then level of surety, that yes, a family was in the making. It made for two months. One evening, things went wrong. I whisked my wife off to the doctor who confirmed that the pregnancy was officially at an end. What had caused it? His official diagnosis was, most probably, toxiplasmosis. Toxopla what?

Toxiplasmosis is an infection that causes premature abortion. One contracts this condition from cat feces and from handling raw meat. The doctor asked if we were meat cutters or had a cat; no to the first but yes to the second. He asked who changed the litter box. My wife was the official litter box changer in my household. Pussycats may well have cost me an heir to my throne; such as it is.

If you are a female who earnestly wants to start a family, a pussycat may not be the pet of choice. Toxoplasmosis is not an endearing trait of the species. Of course, if you are that dilettante teenybopper, perhaps a pussycat is just the thing. Not so endearing charms is, of course, a relative judgment call.

Old Lop

I was just barely out of my teens when I was married for the first time, a situation that should be forbidden by law. I was fresh out of the Marine Corps, conditioned to be filled with hate and general meanness; a state not conducive for marital bliss nor communion with God's lesser creatures. The milk of human kindness gets a little soured by war. Be that as it may, in my impoverished state, my new bride moved into the room provided for me in my parent's house. Among her possessions was a nicely marked, silver gray female tiger cat; as lovely, youthful, and fecund as my new bride.

To this day, I can't remember the cat's name. No matter. Names are human creations, at any rate. Cats will respond to nearly any sound you care to make. "Kitty kitty" is still the universal attention getter. Once in South America, I used this international catcall and found that it worked equally well on Spanish meowing cats. If a tidbit of goodies is at the end of a "kitty kitty", an immediate psychological stimulus response bond takes place. Cats may be opportunists, but they are not stupid.

To keep two bodies and souls together, I had to work several jobs; one of which required me to start my day at four o'clock in the morning. Marriage releases human females from undue displays of affection. The ultimate sacrifice of their bodies justifies any needless further requirements such as getting up with their mates to prepare breakfast at absurd hours. It was a lonely time.

Within a very short time, Kitty, for lack of a better name, came into heat. The entire family, in good Christian manner, was pressed into service to keep Kitty from getting in a family way. We all became guardians of her virtue. Kitty, on the other hand, obviously, could have cared less.

It became a family ritual to provide a chaperoned romp in the diminutive back yard of our Baltimore row house. The first chore was to clear the area of any possible danger. This fell to me; and entailed a search and destroy mission to rid the area of the enemy. The enemy, of course, was an army of assorted tomcats that had been lured to the area by some mysterious scent that was wafted upon the balmy breezes. It never ceased to amaze me that the scent could travel as far and as effectively as it did; and this in competition with the various odors of bus and auto exhaust, thousands of garbage cans and sewers, dogs and birds and God only knows what else, and some quarter of a million humans, many of whom were quite odorous in their own right.

One notable example of the effectiveness of the scent was a particular tom that showed up one day. Amid the array of seemingly unclaimed vagabonds that formed Kitty's entourage of suitors, this one stood out. He was obviously, a gentleman who had gone slumming. Amid his long, golden, Persian tresses, he sported a jeweled collar and a shiny gold nametag. The other street-wise toms batted him about much the same as street urchins victimize the gentry who wander from their protected turf. He didn't even have the savvy to protect himself.

In an act of Christian charity, the family urged that I extricate Little Lord Fauntleroy from the improvised Hell's Angels. With appropriate caution to keep Kitty from seducing our esteemed guest, we read his human identification and contacted his owner; or should I say that we contacted the last human he was willing to share a habitation with. To our surprise, we called a grateful and shocked family who resided on the complete opposite side of Baltimore. How the cat managed to find his way the tens of miles through a major city is a mystery. How the lure of Kitty found him is an even greater mystery. The sex drive that is triggered by this scent is truly amazing. Every male for miles that wants a piece of immortality, or whatever, is miraculously drawn to the spot; a truly amazing bit of olfactory navigation.

I took to my search and destroy missions with a relish. It was a time in my youth when I couldn't rid myself of the memories of pucker-brush and my M-16. With a complete disregard of the pain I inflicted, I removed the enemy with my trusty Daisy BB gun. With my youthful warrior instincts, I could hit a tom that exposed a mere square inch of fur at 50 paces. Those that were willing to hold their ground, I waded into with water and boots. I lofted many a recalcitrant tom with the flair of a place kicker. It was also a time when I had little regard for cats; or anything else for that matter. I think it comes with age.

Once the coast was clear, Kitty was allowed out to romp in the yard. This was always preceded by a sensual role on each step of the porch. She went through contortions, exposing all her feline, feminine wares in a manner that would make most career-minded exotic dancers green with envy. Even with a human perspective, it was obvious what she had on her mind.

There were many toms that came calling. They would awaken the neighborhood at all hours of the night with their internal squabbling during the heat cycle vigil. At any given time, I would reckon at least a dozen. They represented nearly every color and size of cat of which I am aware.

One day, a uniquely grotesque animal made his appearance. He was different in many ways. In shear size alone, he dwarfed all the other toms, which, I might add, dwarfed Kitty. He was as big as a small beagle dog. He walked like a bulldog. He had a massive head that showed the marks of a true campaigner. Lop, as I spontaneously named him, was so named because the tip of his right ear, or the largest part of his right ear fell over. The last half of his ear was in fact, split in two. The edges of both ears were quite uneven; showing the abuse his ears had taken in innumerable encounters.

In addition to his ears, he had a definite scar across his face that skewed the focus of his left eye. When he looked at you, you could never be quite sure with which eye he was staring at you. His coat of fur, I assume, was white. I never saw him in anything other than dirty gray. Several patches of scar tissue were evident. Even the tip of his tail hung at a strange angle. I'm sure it had been broken, or bitten at some point in time and had never mended properly. All in all, he was the most incredible tom I had ever seen or have seen to this day.

In spite of his looks, he was a most congenial animal. My search and destroy missions became singularly focused upon Lop. He endured the Daisy fusillade with only a mild grimace. Water of nearly any temperature was only a minor annoyance. It had the effect of turning his fur a shade or two lighter. It took a hefty place kick just to get his attention.

Even with all this abuse, he never seemed to loose his catly good nature. When I would approach him with criminal intent just prior to my abuse, he would stand there and break into a motor-like purr of remarkable racket. Several times when I had occasion to enter the house from the rear, I had to pass through the tomcat picket line. Old Lop would rub against my legs as if we were old friends. When I would get up early in the morning, he would be staring through the window. I thought he had a gargantuan nerve, and would abuse him that much more.

Over time, I began to grow attached to Lop. He was persistent, brave, and friendly. He took the abuse like a man. He was a man's man; or cat in this instance. In spite of my mission, I developed a real affection for him; not as a cat, but as a fellow male mortal. We were frustrated warriors of a sort; and I understood him.

Kitty's heat cycle seemed to go on for months rather than days. One fateful day, with the entire family as a witness, Kitty's heat cycle ended abruptly. With all the preliminary caution of past romps, I went for a search and destroy mission. Thap! Thap! I sent two loitering toms in fast flight. Lop was nowhere to be seen. The coast appeared to be clear. Kitty made her lurid entry into the yard. She rolled and slithered her way down each step, seductively, very slowly, one step at a time. When she reached the bottom step, from seemingly out of nowhere, an enormous gray fur ball popped out from beneath the bottom step. Biff, bam, thank you ma'am! Kitty and Lop were "married" in the space of time it took the family to gasp and make a run for the door. By the time we got it open and landed on the first step, it was all over. Lop bounded off in a leisurely saunter, never to be seen again. Kitty just continued her seductive rolling; the act now attributed to a brazen hussy.

I could never understand how Lop could have hidden his enormous carcass under the bottom step. Also, did he have the problem solving cunning to set up the ambush? With hindsight, I can truthfully say that even while it was happening I found some perverse pleasure. If any tom was to deflower Kitty, Lop was my choice. I had developed a deep affection for him in a weird sort of way. "That's my man!"

Several weeks later, Kitty gave birth to six little Lops in the corner of my closet, no less. Lop had gotten his piece of immortality. A tomcat's mission in life is to procreate. Lop was a true survivor. How many other Kitties he "married" defy the imagination. His genes are, no doubt, still in the gene pool of Baltimore alleycatdom.

I can't remember what ever happened to Kitty or the kittens. We, no doubt, found homes for them all. The inner city absorbs all manner of kittens, pups, people, and cockroaches in a never-ending supply. The inner city does not produce pedigree stock. This is reserved for the know-nothing gentry. What the inner city does produce is the hardened survivor; a truly American pedigree. Man or beast is hardened in the cauldron of the fittest. Old Lop was one of the fittest.

Out on a Limb

People too often attribute human frailties to animals. If they were that frail, they wouldn't have survived the million or so odd years to take up residence with people. What's more, they did it without several thousand years of Judeo Christian ethics. Cats stand in the top ten of my survival of the fittest list; others being houseflies, mosquitoes, ants, cockroaches, Norway rats, pigeons, mice, English sparrows, and starlings. You'll notice that these are animals that can "cut it" in the city. Anyone can survive in the country. The rural environs are anachronisms. They are residual bits and pieces of a different era of human existence. The city, in all its forms, is the blueprint for man's marvelous, or frightening, future. Cats are masters at our own game.

The one thing that you don't have in great numbers in the city is, of course, trees. Not that they aren't there. They are. They may be isolated, disjointed and even dismembered; but they are there. The future may see them replaced by plastic telephone poles, but they serve the same function that they have served for millennia: perches and nurseries for starlings, relief stations for dogs, and emergency escape routes for cats. Like their cousins the leopards, pussycats take refuge in trees.

I always recall the children' story that I heard as a youngster about the discussion between a fox and a cat. The fox was bragging about how he was called cunning because he had a hundred different tricks to evade the pack of dogs. The poor, embarrassed cat admitted that he had only one. When the pack of hounds descended upon them, the fox employed all hundred of them but could not evade the dogs. The cat did his one thing and ran up a tree. They really are tree animals of sorts.

I wonder to what extent Hollywood is responsible for the image of cats stranded in trees. I've seen a number of movies where either the hero or the fire department is required to rescue the heroine's pussycat that was chased up a tree by a dog. Dogs never seem to acquire the reputation of a "heavy" for this fete of villainy. Let one cat get caught riding a witch's broom and the whole of catdom is condemned. Talk about a double standard. To racism and sexism must be added: petism. Fire Departments still answer calls to rescue errant cats up trees.

I personally don't believe rescue is required. I've spent innumerable hours in the woods, have lived in the country most of my life, have had many cats of my own and have watched the antics of many who weren't mine. I say "mine" with some sense of realism, of course. In all that time, I have never found a stranded cat in the rural areas; or worse, the mortal remains of one stuck in a tree. Am I the only one who has had this experience; or am I so callous that I am blind to reality? Certainly Hollywood wouldn't fabricate a lie. Come to think of it, I've never seen a talking rabbit in the woods either; but then I don't travel in the same crowds as do Hollywood stars.

I grew up in the city thinking that cats have this sort of weak mindedness to go up trees without having the foresight or physical prowess to get back down. My wife who had an even more sheltered life also believed in this myth. It was the sacred responsibility of all cat owners to feed them special canned cat food, provide a comfortable pillow bed, check for fleas and climb trees to rescue them at frequent intervals. If one is male and married, it naturally falls to him. Him was me when I had my first personal experience with an honest to goodness cat up a tree crisis during the first year of my marriage. Gladys, who I mentioned before, was the instrument of my education.

Behind our Hansel and Gretel country home, there were two enormous Norway spruce trees. They framed our home, provided shade for the back porch and filled my rainspouts with spruce needles. They were gorgeous creatures, if I may take liberty with the word. The dogs and cats lived amiably in a giant fur ball in the dry dirt nestled among the protruding roots at the base of the trees. Summer or winter, there was always a pulsating ball of hair of indistinguishable genus and specie either asleep or just resting beneath their whistling branches. It was idyllic.

One day when I returned home from work, we heard the pathetic meow of Gladys from a direction that we were unaccustomed to hearing her. She was well up the largest of the trees; perched on one of the labyrinth of branches. It was obvious that there would be no coaxing her from her precarious perch. It was citified pilgrim to the rescue. I donned my work clothes, set up my ladder that was too short by double its length, conjured up a tremendous case of male chauvinist piggism and artificial bravado and climbed among the limbs to rescue the fair feline damsel in distress. God, how I hate heights. After several lacerations received from my ungrateful damsel, I dislodged her from her branch and carried her to safety; mostly mine, thank heaven.

I had performed the fourth commandment of cat ownership successfully. With the exception of throbbing scratches, the evening went on uneventfully. Why had she taken refuge in the trees? I certainly never noticed any problem with the dogs. They were old shoes; and I was sure that Gladys, who was a good tenth their size, could turn any one or both of them into a shredded, quivering coward. They were already the latter.

The next day, lo and behold, the pathetic cry greeted me again. Again, Captain Nice to the service of God and cat! It was with less zeal I might add. I hoped that this wasn't the raison d'etat of having cats. I had been raised in the inner city. As the comedian Red Skelton so aptly put it: "I lived in the ghetto before it caught on." The scarcity of climbable trees in the inner city was suddenly seen as a virtue of civilization.

As I drove home the following day, I was concerned as to what I would find. It had been, as I recall, a "rough day at the office". I was a schoolteacher of 12 to 15 year olds; and believe me, a rough day in a junior high school is a rough day. A financial crisis at General Motors is a minor annoyance in comparison. I was in no mood for climbing among branches and being sliced to ribbons for doing a good deed. I was in the mood for a bad deed to soothe the savage beast. Sure enough, meow, meow from above. "Tough you little dummy, I'm in no mood for your stupidity. I'll get you later."

I had an uncomfortable dinner. Between the pathetic "meows" and my wife's description of my hard heartedness, I became cynical about the whole affair. In that it would be the same thing tomorrow, why not leave Gladys up there until tomorrow. Then we could feed her enough to last her for a two-day rescue cycle rather than an every day rescue. My wife couldn't, or rather wouldn't, see the logic in that scheme. I tried some other delaying tactic. It was dinnertime for the animals. Gladys had already missed the begging time at dinner. I'm sure that was what all the meowing was about.

When I took the food out to the animals, there was the customary mad jockeying for position. There were always animal guests for these feedings. At least one of my neighbor-to-the-south's cats and one of my neighbor to-the-east's dogs managed to show up at dinnertime. They had to find their own place but give 'way to the hosts'. I heard a flurry of activity among the branches. Gladys couldn't believe that we would start without her. I watched her descend. It wasn't the most graceful descent; but she did get down without the aide of Mr. Niceguy.

The ultimate truth I learned that day is: When they get hungry enough, they'll come down. I've never rescued another pussycat from a tree since. I admit that I've known a kitten to stay up for over twenty-four hours. A kind hearted, artsy-craftsy, 1960's lady who is a self proclaimed cat person rescued the stranded kitty. I merely held the ladder. I was convinced that even this energetic gesture wasn't required. Considering my fear of heights and my knowledge of pussycats, I'll never go out on a limb again. Not figuratively or literally.

⁇
One Man's Meat

Is there anyone who could refuse broiled lobster dipped in melted butter? How about a filet mignon cooked to perfection and smothered in buttered mushrooms? While it may be difficult to believe, the answer is yes. Some poor benighted souls would refuse these tantalizing feasts. Just writing about them makes me hungry. I know one person who absolutely hates lobster; and another who would rather have a hot dog than a steak. Then of course, there are the vegetarians who look down on us meat eaters as if we were cannibals consuming our fellow mortal beings. There is just no pleasing some people. One just can't predict the dietary preference of people. Nor of cats, I might add.

According to all the comics and movies, cats are supposed to like fish, milk and raw meat. Is there a newspaper comic strip that hasn't shown some pussycat either being treated to a fish dinner or being chased from one by a merchant? The theme is as old as I am; and that covers a few years. The discovery of paper predates me by only a few years. More than one veterinarian has told me that raw fish is really not good for cats. I honestly don't know. Several of my cats dive right in when I have tossed them some squirming, flopping fish. I shudder just remembering the crunching of the bones.

But then, I have had other cats that look at me like I have questioned the legitimacy of their parentage when I have offered them a fish. They would have nothing to do with it, much less eat one of those slimy things.

The same unimpeachable source suggests that cats thrive on saucers of milk. The milkman's unguarded quart of delivered milk is a common target of some pesky cat. These cartoonists are obviously as old as I. There are just too few milk delivery men left in America to even give meaning to the vast number of youthful comic strip readers. I haven't seen a milk truck or a quart of milk in front of someone's door in a coon's age. The integrity of our fellow citizens has deteriorated to the point that one does not leave something of value, no matter how little, unguarded and at risk. We have gone beyond a time when just the milk would be stolen. Now, the milk truck itself would be stolen no sooner than the milkman left it.

But cats did like those broken quart bottles of milk during the heyday of milkmen. On cold winter days, the freezing milk would push the cream up beyond the bottle tops like a natural frozen custard machine. It provided golden opportunities for those alley cats that haunted the early morning hours with the milkmen and us newspaper delivery boys.

But then, I have seen some cats that wouldn't drink milk if they were dying of thirst. I have put some cats' noses in the milk so long that the emission of bubbles in the milk suggested that they were drowning; and they still wouldn't drink it. I have had some knowledgeable cat people say that milk is bad for cats. Again, I really don't know. Those inner city alley cats sure scarfed it down; and they were never sick. Maybe it's only bad for those inbred pedigree pansies that never had the thrill of knocking over an inner city garbage can. There is just no accounting for taste.

Raw meat is a universal cat food. It would be most uncatly if any pussy that calls himself or herself a pussycat would refuse raw meat. Most go wild over meat. Even my friendliest pussies didn't know how to conduct themselves civilly when given a piece of liver or chunk of steak. The dichotomous friend-enemy relationship that exists between man and cat comes to the fore. They take the meat and then growl with each chew. A sort of high octave growl wowl wowl wowl is emitted paralleling the mastication until the meat is gone. Try to take it back and you'll see who or what is nearest and dearest to pussycat. You'll always come in second to a piece of liver. You shouldn't let this hurt your feelings, however; all things even out. Some cats come in second to a light colored rug.

In truth, while all cats eat their share of protein through meat and meat by-products, some cats have their own personal and quite unique preferences for the most uncatly food one could imagine. The cat that shared my first home, Gladys, had a yen for grasshoppers. It certainly was not because I starved her and she had to resort to eating such unlikely delights. We have never been guilty of having a skinny cat. On the contrary! Gladys truly seemed to relish grasshoppers. I'm sure they were marvelous playthings for the first one or two. But after she tried one, she acquired a taste for them. Not only did she catch a disproportionate share on her own; it was a real treat when I would catch one and feed it to her like a potato chip. Like potato chips, she could never stop with just one.

Amos, a young tiger tom that was thrust into our life, somehow was "turned on" to pizza. I remember that we thought it cute when he began to eat the remnants of our midnight pizza snacks. We tested the extent of his pizza preference by offering him bigger and bigger pieces. In no time, he was consuming a whole slice along with the rest of us. With a pregnant wife and a pizza parlor only a half a block away, Amos ate a lot of pizza. I don't mean he ate the cheese off the top. He ate the whole thing, including the crusts that we didn't eat. Amos loved pizza.

My niece and her husband had been adopted by a transient tabby of considerable age. They called her Checkers, but didn't share the origin of the name. She was nearly toothless and had the square face of an old cat. Checkers had a pleasant disposition; but, like most old people, she had little tolerance for hyperactive children; especially human children who were many times more noisy and troublesome than kittens. Her belly sagged as if she had created quite a few of the latter in her misspent youth.

Sometime during her life, she had developed a partiality for Oreo cookies. In fact, given her choice of liver, steak or an Oreo, she would take the cookie every time. My wife, the daughter of a dentist, suggested that is the reason for Checkers' rather obvious lack of teeth. I'm sure she didn't brush after all that sugar. I, for one, wouldn't try to brush a cat's teeth! I doubt he would take kindly to such civilized abuse.

There must be something to the sugar theory. The only other toothless pussycat I know of belongs to the office manager of my former employer. Her cat, Myrtle, has a "thing" for a very particular thing. It seems she developed a taste for Duncan Hines' strawberry cake.

Like humans, cats have a number of bizarre food preferences. Most people think I'm weird when I go out of my way to get Brussels sprouts. Why shouldn't pussycats have their "off the wall" specialty? What's one man's meat is another man's poison, . . or grasshopper, or pizza, or Oreo, or Duncan Hines' strawberry cake.

My Fat Little Sister

Samantha wasn't really my cat. In that she was my mother's cat, she was, by some strange quirk of animal relationship, my little step sister; my fat little sister to be sure. On my frequent visits back home as all newly independent fledglings make, I would naturally tease my remaining siblings. Upon greeting my family and raiding the refrigerator, I next enjoyed a caustic quip about the increasing girth of Samantha. In that I was now an expatriate of the household and didn't enjoy nuclear status, I was promptly vehemently attacked by my mother and younger brother, Tim. They came to her defense with a partisan passion that clouded the truth. Samantha was fat! Their denial didn't change matters. What God hath joined together, man's euphemisms could not put asunder, and all that. In hindsight, I believe they were as serious as I was not. It's difficult to leave home gracefully.

Samantha didn't come to live with me until the latter years of her life. Most of her life was spent in my mother's and brother's homes. In that Tim was a career military man, his houses were quite different and changed frequently. The escapades of my little sister growing up were related to me by my brother. Mind you, he is a cat man, so his judgment is skewed. He thinks cats are people.

My younger brother who, while not admitting to being a true cat person, signed his latest Christmas card: Tim, Belen, Mildred, Tiger, Marie, Salt. The first three I recognized as my brother, my sister-in-law, and my niece. The last three, I'm sure, are three step cats that have joined his family. In that I haven't seen my brother for several years, it takes some getting used to adjust to these feline relatives. But then, I'm not a true cat person. To Tim, there is no distinction in genus.

As all siblings get jealous of the disparate attention that their parents bestow on their brothers and sisters, so too, in a perverted sort of way, did I. Even though Samantha was a cat and even though I was a young adult, I felt that she partook of the goodies of life far greater than was offered to me. She really did. To quote the oft-used cliché: Mom loved her better than she loved me. Now you think that I'm kidding, don't you? I will plead my case and allow you to judge.

First, when I was growing up, food was something my older brother and I were not allowed to waste. "Think of the poor starving children in Europe", my mother would hammer us with. Growing up in the World War II era, this argument would drive us to patriotic mea culpa's. If this weren't enough, we were raised in an Irish Catholic neighborhood where we were made to feel guilty about everything. If I didn't eat all my spinach, the nuns would remind me that I was personally driving the nails deeper into Christ's hands and feet. Is it any wonder that I have an inferiority complex? It was interesting that years later, I met a charming lady from Denmark who was raised during the same era. She was chastised with: "Think of the poor starving Indians in America". I guess all parents have a geographic ruse for making their children feel guilty for not eating. In any event, I couldn't waste food. We didn't have that much as I remember; and what we had was rationed.

Samantha, my mother's favorite, was allowed to pick and choose, accept and reject. I would have gotten a swat with a yardstick if I had exhibited the slightest hint of being finicky. Samantha, on the other hand, made Morris, the TV cat food star, look like an uncouth slob. Sam took finickyness to its greatest heights. She would have another and yet another can opened until she discovered something that she had a catly yen for. Samantha could waste food.

Second, which grew out of the first, leftovers were the logical follow up to firstovers. When I was growing up, if we had mashed potatoes on day one, day two was sure to be followed with potato cakes. If we had chicken, and only rarely I might add, it was followed by cold chicken and hot gravy on day two and chicken soup on day three. There were no exceptions. It was a less affluent world in which I was raised.

My fat little sister, however, was raised in good times. If those cans I mentioned were rejected, they were, more often than not, discarded. "The refrigerator dries out the food", my mother would protest. Heck, as long as it was restorable by a generous soaking over night, it was good enough for my older brother and me. Samantha never ate leftovers.

Third, with the termination of my baby food, no other foods were bought just to please me. Once past the junior food stage, I got what the family got. "What, you don't want to eat turnips and kidneys? Then you go without eating, young man! Think of the poor starving . .", well you know the rest. Turnips and kidneys when you are a six year old? Icchht! God, how I learned to hate Europeans.

Samantha, on the other hand, always had special treats. There were few prepared cat foods that Samantha would tolerate. My mother would arrange her shopping trips to exotic distant super markets to access these choice foods. I personally would rather eat the worst can of cat food rather than turnips and kidneys. What is more, to provide a pleasant alternative to the choice cat food, canned tuna and even canned shrimp was added to my fat little sister's larder. With no remorse or sense of guilt, I confess that when I ran across a left-over can of shrimp in the refrigerator, I scarfed it down just as fast as I could. Mother never bought me shrimp.

Now do you believe me? Have I convinced you that mother loved Samantha better than she did me? The data are incontrovertible. Maybe Samantha got the lion's share of affection because, technically, she was the youngest. The youngest always get special consideration. My younger brother also shared in the better life of the family's increasing affluence. Maybe too, it was because she was the only girl in my mother's inventory of children. Mom was the old fashioned kind of girl that lost her identity in a household of boys and men. I always thought my mother wished that I were a girl rather than a troublesome boy.

The most probable reason Samantha was so indulged was the fact that she was a pussycat. Let's face it. Everybody goes ga ga over a pussycat. Samantha really was a remarkable animal. In spite of her preferential treatment, I loved her too; even though I never missed a chance to steal her shrimp and make some sarcastic remark about her size. I knew she didn't hold it against me. I'm not so sure about my mother and little brother. Several years later, because of a game of family musical houses, Sam came to live with me. I could never treat her as just another cat. She was always my fat little sister.

The Sorehead

Since childhood, I had the concept that all cats are the natural enemies of birds. Being raised in the city, this meant that forty percent of all non human beings in the neighborhood were the mortal enemy of forty percent of the remaining beings. The other twenty percent constituted the dogs, goldfish and unowned vermin of the inner city. Nothing as exotic as a cow or chicken can be found in the city's core. My neighborhood was no different.

Because we shared our homes and garbage cans with the cats and our stale bread and birdbaths with the birds, both were considered neighbors. Life was hard enough; so we had difficulty as kids in understanding this violent relationship. Because birds were so innocuous, pussycats became identified with our earliest concepts of villainy. While none of the local cats actually made a kill, the neighborhood truths had it that someone heard from someone over on such and such street that so and so's cat caught a young sparrow; and, had it not been for the Christian interference of so and so's mother, the cat would have killed that bird. That was good enough for me! Cats were villains when it came to birds.

Over the years, I've come to grips with the life and death struggle birds wage against cats. It's in their natures, so I've become immune to this seeming violation of Christian love and humanitarian respect for life. But then, I don't know any Christian or human cats. I've known some to approach this goal; even more than the number of Christian humans that have approached the goal. I have come to accept the natural law of predator prey relationship as much as I've come to accept crime and war. Over my lifetime, humans have managed to kill several tens of millions of other humans both violently and needlessly. I'm sure the number of birds that have met a violent end from pussycats is but a small fraction of this number. Talk about getting "bad press!" Just as the death of a back yard bird is no more of a story than a man being bitten by a dog; "Bird strikes back" is as much of a story as "Man bites dog". It is such a rare occurrence that it must surely be news. But, does it happen in real life?

As part of the duties of one of my jobs, I traveled all over the country to work with teams of technical writers. I met many interesting people in many interesting parts of the nation. One such interesting experience was in Phoenix, Arizona. I was invited to see the house of one of the technical writers. It was a magnificent modern suburban home built in the Spanish architectural style. In the blazing summer sun of the desert, it was cool and bright. The back yard was the typical Spanish or Roman garden, a sort of atrium where the entrance to the house was the entrance to the garden, with living quarters surrounding the garden. My host and his charming wife gave me the tour and introduced me to the family.

One of the family members was a furry, not quite pedigree, reddish Persian cat. On the top of his head, I was warned, was a gooey medical cream. He had a boo boo on his bean. In point of fact, he had a serious, open head wound. The vet had assured my hosts that any further irritation or injury could be fatal. The pussycat was the victim of neighborhood bullies.

In the house, pussy was a gentle, pet type pussycat. Outside, he was reduced to a cowed, cringing shell of a cat. It seems that a husband and wife mockingbird couple had decided to take up residence in the neighborhood. Not waiting to see what kind of neighbor their fuzzy familiar would be, they heeded the bad press and their natural bigotry and decided that there was no room in the neighborhood for the cat. Mockingbirds, being known for their not so nice dispositions, took the offensive to make the older resident feel like a persecuted minority in his own home.

As the story was related to me, in the spring of that year, the cat was living his usual benign life of walking in the garden and going to the potty under the trumpet vines when the birds began their dive bombing and strafing runs at him. The stunned pussycat took to a swiping defense that made matters worse. Mockingbirds respond to violence with increased violence. They battered the cat that lost the battle as well as his dignity. His reputation as a bird-killing villain was lost in a split head and a splitting headache. From then until that time in late summer when I was introduced to that pathetic mock feline coward, he had taken that serious abuse every time he needed to relieve himself during daylight hours. I inquired whether he ever tried to catch the birds. It appeared that he had lost all his sense of individuality in the way prisoners of war become dispirited. He just took the abuse.

I witnessed a frantic foray to the outdoor litter box. The poor cat looked up and down for what seemed to be an eternity to make sure the birds were not in sight. I was told that they always knew. The cat didn't make five feet into the open before the first mockingbird sortie was flown. Swish, bang, a direct hit on the old noggin! For a couple of seconds, the cat scrambled in every direction to avoid the onslaught, but, without a plan of escape, managed to go nowhere. He just rolled over and meowed; more "ow'''d then "me'''d. What a disgusting picture. Here was one of nature's true killers pleading with two birds in an incomprehensible meow to be left alone. He couldn't even go the sand box in peace.

To ad insult to injury, the male bird didn't even bother to fly very far away to make his stand. He alighted no more than four feet away from the cat and pranced around as if to herd him into position. The cat wouldn't even look the bird in the eyes. He avoided direct eye contact like the plague. He was beat, and the bird knew it. The lady of the house had to escort her pansy pussy to the trumpet vine to maintain his regularity. Surely, he was giving catdom a bad reputation. His poor little bladder took a beating when the humans weren't at home. The underside of an opaque topped coffee table became the daytime prison for the cat for most of the summer. While as a kid I felt sorry for the birds who where chased by cats, I must say that the strings of my heart were plucked by that pathetic reversal I encountered in Phoenix.

Technical writing projects don't last forever, so I lost contact with my host for some time. It was more than a year later before we met at an industry function. After several drinks and some small talk, I inquired of the health of his pussycat, whose name I obviously can't remember. He laughed, and the conversation drifted far enough distant to rouse intense curiosity in me. I pushed him again on the subject. He informed me that one afternoon it seems that the mockingbird got too cocky and too close. The coward suddenly got a shot in the arm, or paw in this case, of primitive catly courage and made a meal of the neighborhood bully. Steeled by this success and filled with the sense of retribution, pussy also ate his nemesis' wife within twenty-four hours. I only assume that at that late date in the summer, the bird's children were long gone from the neighborhood.

Not that I still don't profess to have Christian love and humanist respect for life; nor sympathize with the plight of the poor bird as one of nature's underdogs, or underbirds as the case may be. It is just that I had real empathy for that poor, sorehead cat. We feel very uncomfortable when our truths and natural laws are questioned. Cats go after birds. That is an unfortunate but comfortable law of life. I felt good that Sorehead restored my sense of stability in an imperfect world.

Stuff It

The range of noises that a human can utter is absolutely amazing. He can make a sound to emulate anything from a bird to a motorcycle and nearly everything in between. I get a kick out of listening to very young children experiment with new sounds. It surprises even them to discover the vast array of non-human noises. Machine guns, automobiles, jet airplanes, and, most importantly, nearly any other animal on this planet is well within the purview of man.

I regularly hold conversations with my cat, Bob, in catese. I don't have the slightest idea of what I'm saying in catese, but Bob talks back to me as if it is clear to him. Cats are somewhat limited in their perceived vocabulary. Variations on a theme of "meow" are a rather limiting way to go through life. It must force them to communicate in some form other than language. It also means that they have no way of being deceptive. Can you imagine a world where one can't deceive or lie? What would lawyers and politicians do? Yes, a varied language is a necessary form of human survival.

One of the sounds that I reveled in throughout my life is the whistle. I can "slow" whistle. By this I mean that I can expel air across my puckered lips and make a piccolo sound. Very early on, I amused myself with all sorts of musical scores; some original. As the score in "The King and I" stated so well, whenever I felt afraid, I whistled a happy tune. At four o'clock in the morning delivering newspapers on a dark street, it did raise my spirits. What is more, sound has a way of becoming amplified at that period just before dawn. With no other sound, I sounded like a genuine mono-noted calliope. I loved it.

Whistling seems to have become a lost art. None of the younger children in my present neighborhood whistle. I suppose that they think computers and boom boxes have a monopoly on making sound. I whistled all the time. My mother often made the statement that she would lie in bed awake while waiting for my return from my adolescent escapades. When she heard me whistling from several blocks off, she new I was safe and returning. She would fall off to sleep before I ever arrived at the door. Mind you, she never told me when I was young enough and devious enough to take advantage of that fact. I would have whistled my lungs out at the beginning of the block until she went to sleep and then stayed out to raise Cain with my buddies. Sometimes my buddies and I would whistle three or more part harmony.

I never learned to "hard" whistle. By this I mean the type of shrill whistle you hear on cowboy movies. It is the kind you use if you really want to get attention. I secretly envied those individuals who make that marvelous sound. Not that I didn't try. Believe me; I practiced until my lips were numb. The only sound I could ever muster was a dumb noise akin to a leaky tire valve. It was downright embarrassing. I was and am never to know the joy or even a fantasy of a herd of cattle picking up their gait in response to my whistling prods. A herd of steers laughing at me for making my absurd sound is not a pleasant thought.

It is even more embarrassing to admit that I married a willowy, very feminine lady who can blast my eardrums with her cowboy whistle. She learned it from her mother who is every bit as good. Being out cowboyed by a girl is one thing. Being out cowboyed by a willowy, feminine seventy five year old lady is downright cruel!

Whistling is used by humans to call their animal friends. Dogs are uniformly receptive to responding to whistles. Cats, not known for their eagerness to be controlled by anything or any body, do not respond. If Pavlov had used cats rather than beagles, stimulus response bonding psychology would have been a Madison Avenue discovery. Morris is a prime example of a cat's response to external control. We have no way of knowing what our animals think about whistling. We only know that they respond.

Gladys, my first cat after moving to the country, responded to whistling. She obviously didn't care for it. At least she gave every indication that she didn't. I was still young enough and happy enough to break out into a whistle while in casual reading or paper work. Gladys would run over to me and put her face on my chin and shove just as hard as she could. If that failed to shut me up, she would stick her face right in my mouth, as if her snoot was a cork. That always worked.

The first time it happened I was surprised. After that, it got to be a game. I would whistle just to tease her. Pavlov, eat your heart out! I got a cat to respond with a stimulus. It worked every time. She couldn't have communicated any more clearly if she had mastered a human language. What she was saying was: "Stuff it!"

David R. Torrence

Traveling Companions

The city and suburbs at four o'clock in the morning is a different world than the same sites at four o'clock in the afternoon. If you are a recluse and desire to avoid humanity, live your life from midnight 'till sunrise. You'll get the impression that you are one of the few people in an antimatter world. It is the world of the hobo: the human hobo just passing through, the hobo dogs who, like their human counterparts, are just passing through or who have lost their people, and the true owner of the world of urban darkness, the hobo pussycats; most of whom were kicked out of their comfortable human abode to roam the streets loving and fighting with their pussycat buddies and gals.

When I was a young boy, like so many inner city youths of that time, I delivered morning newspapers to earn spending money. For a twelve year old, the world of the wee morning hours is lonely and a little frightening. Tales of criminals, deviants, drunks and assorted kooks weighed heavily on a young mind even at that comparatively safe period in history. Today, the criminals, deviants, drunks and assorted kooks seem to have won the day. They do indeed rule the darkened streets of the inner city today. Back then, however, it was mostly fear of the dark and the silence that preyed upon the innocent.

It is my blessing or curse, depending upon one's point of view, to have a natural kinship with pussycats and puppy dogs; actually, with any animal. I have been known to get along just swell with wild skunks and assorted vermin. I hope this is not symbolic of something. They like me for some reason. Maybe it is because I like them. The old adage is: "To have a friend, you have to be a friend". When it comes to animals, I guess I'm perceived as friendly.

On all of my paper routes, I was fortunate enough to run into one or several of the aforementioned doggy hobos who, desirous of friendly company, would accompany me the many blocks and neighborhoods of my appointed rounds. This was a symbiotic relationship. I lost all fear of the criminals, deviants, drunks and assorted kooks, real or imaginary, when accompanied by my faithful army of friends. Some looked quite imposing. Others were probably tagging along with me to alleviate their own fear of the dark.

As I look back upon this time of my life, I truly can't remember very many days that I did not have a canine entourage. I would pick up recruits at each new block. Somehow, a sort of truce among strangers existed among the pack. They were allowed to join or desert without so much as a bark or scowl. I would just make a friendly greeting to a surprised newcomer or transient and he or she would just fall in cadence; often joining the merry band at the same time the following morning. They were good company. We made no demands upon each other. We just shared quiet companionship. In point of fact, I probably had more hours of positive socializing with the dogs than I had with my human counterparts in the controlled and contrived school environment of that time. I know I liked the dogs more than some of my teachers and classmates.

I had a number of different routes at different times during these years. One route was in a brand new suburban neighborhood. It was the period after World War II when housing developments were going up at a rate exceeded only by the developer's ability to create names for the projects. Every conceivable English word was coupled with "wood" to form the marketable name for another paradise in which to bring up a crop of postwar children or a failed attempt at getting a draft deferment. Ten years later, the same words were attached to "gate" to name another round of building. The route, comprising the houses and apartments of Northwood, Lockwood, Bellwood and Edgewood, bordered a large wooded area that served as the major camping area for the city's Boy Scout Camperee. Today, it is considered part of the inner city with many high-rise buildings far beyond the city's former border with the known universe.

It was a particularly dark route. The city's municipal lighting system was still miles behind the feverish pace of new building. The only lights available for nighttime navigation was from a few exit lights from the laundry rooms at the ends of the apartment buildings and the outside door lights inadvertently left on by a late arrival. Because it was so dark and because it was on the city's border with the great-uncivilized wilderness, the paper route was especially threatened by the hobgoblins of the unknown. It was a fearful route.

Fortunately for me, my Pied Piper personality turned up a couple of unlikely but welcomed companions for my lonely hours. One was a black and brown fuzzy faced mutt that could have been a stand in for the movie star: Bengie. He latched on to me, or rather we latched on to each other, in the first block of my new adventure. I never discovered who owned him or where he lived. He became a permanent companion for the several years that I had the route. For the several morning hours, I owned him. At the end of my route, we parted amicably to pursue our separate daytime lives.

My other unlikely partner was a tan and white tomcat. Mutt and I encountered him in the fifth block of my route. Normally, cats were secretive creatures that hid or ran from my merry bands. In this case, Mutt and I didn't present much of a threat. Tom, so named for lack of imagination, was nearly as large as Mutt, again similarly named. Even without my customary greeting, Tom trooped in and became a fellow traveler. Mutt, being a liberal Christian of dogism persuasion , didn't show any racial, ethnic or even genus or species discrimination. We were all God's early morning hours' creatures.

139

One of the complaints cat haters have is that cats are not like dogs; an obvious but not ingenious observation. They complain that dogs will go for walks with you while cats won't. My charge to them, while not original, is: "Seek and ye shall find". There are cats who aren't a tinker's darn different than dogs in most of their actions. Tom was one. He was so doglike that when we encountered new, temporary canine recruits along the way, they made no discriminatory gesture about that "other kid" either.

Tom taught me Christian love and forgiveness. This was during a period in my life when I was an avid if not successful hunter. From my other adult hunters, I was filled with the poison of hate for cats. "Cats killed game!" The absence of rabbits and game birds was caused entirely by pussycats. The entire world knew that. If it was good enough for the entire world, it was good enough for me. Pussycats were the reason I spent so many hours in the woods without seeing game; not because there were other hunters spaced every fifty yards apart and they shot everything that moved from sparrow to field mouse. We were not to blame. It was the nighttime predation of pussycats. Doubt did creep into my worldly truths. I too was a creature of the nighttime. The only real thing I ever saw pussycats prey upon were the herds of loose lid garbage cans that were more prolific and productive in the inner city jungle than in the barren countryside. Cats aren't stupid.

When I first encountered Tom, I must admit I abused him. I shot him with the rubber bands I used to secure the papers. I would periodically "bean" him with a thrown paper when he perched himself on a customer's porch. I was generally nasty to this archenemy of all hunters and the rest of natural life. He accepted my abuses and repaid them with loyalty and companionship. There was not a mean streak in his body. At the ripe old age of twelve, I began questioning the truths of this world and began a whole set of my own truths which have defied the greater society ever since. I made peace with Tom and all pussycatdom in the wee hours of the morning without the din of human truths and social pressure. He was a better creature than I.

Bob, the cat who is presently wrestling with a golf ball on my kitchen floor is another one of those people loving cats to the point of being a traveling companion. When we take walks around the neighborhood, he accompanies us. Every one of our neighbors knows Bob. He visits them unannounced regularly; a slight breech of etiquette. This is the age of the suburban walker and jogger. Bob accompanies my neighbors on their healthful rounds. He seems to enjoy the company of people. Cats can be good traveling companions.

David R. Torrence

Avoiding and Voiding

How or why humanity started down the road to deny our animal nature is an eternal puzzlement to me. We seem to become embarrassed at the most minor exhibition of our bodily functions. Animals get rid of their liquid and solid wastes. People get rid of their liquid and solid wastes. Humans, however, go to great lengths to put this normal, healthy function in some sort of ritualistic limbo. I've heard and read of people who have experienced a great deal of physical discomfort and psychological trauma relating to this common, mammalian function. If it weren't for medical objectivity, we probably wouldn't have any acceptable polite words for it in our language.

It is true that we just can't "void" any place and any time we have the urge. It is a crowded world. We could come to grips with reality, on the other hand. At a restaurant, whatever do the ladies do when they go to powder their noses? Come on now! Everyone knows that they are not going to powder their noses. The gentlemen go the rest room. Again, get a grip! They are not going there to rest. One, I've never ever seen a couch or soft chair in a men's room in the hundreds if not thousands of men's rooms that I've frequented in my lifetime. Even if they contained furniture, what kind of person would want to take a nap in a men's room anyway? So, why do we call them powder rooms and rest rooms? Are we applying euphemisms to deny our natures? You bet!

Pets, being fellow mortals, also "void". For those humans who get embarrassed over these events, perhaps a pussycat is the pet of choice. Unlike dogs that make grotesque gestures and perform absurd gyrations to accomplish their needs, cats do it in style. A typical event for a dog would consist of "telegraphing" his or her intent with an obvious sniffing out the appropriate spot. Dogs just don't do it anywhere. What ever their logic, they have to do it in just the right spot. You know when they have found it. I've watched my many canine charges with bladders bulging make a hasty olfactory sweep for the proper place. When found, they put on the brakes and circle the spot like a golf pro sizing up the putt. Ahh! The powder room, of sorts! When completed, a good sniff to gather some sort of canine data completes the process. A few vigorous scratches to make a charade of burying the mess are optional. This is, no doubt, some sort of doggy bureaucratic gesture to cover their butt; or the effluence thereof.

Pussycats, on the other hand, do not cause their human overlords to turn red with embarrassment or green with disgust. The pussycat's elimination process is downright elegant in animal terms. Unless one is an astute pussycat watcher, one would never know that the event is happening. The only telltale signs are an uncharacteristic curl of the tail, a slightly more erect bearing, and an obvious expression of ecstasy on their face. They make it look like it is an orgasmic experience; but not for publication. They actually bury their discharge; no government jobs in pussycatdom.

Pussycats are naturals for those humans with sensitive natures or weak stomachs. While unabashed in many ways, when it comes to their bodily activities, they are modest, clean, and discrete. They avoid the embarrassment of voiding.

🐾

Growing Old

As I not so gracefully grow old, I think back to the times my mother would join me when, each morning, I would look out from the kitchen door and survey my realm. She would put her arm around my waist, hug me and sermonize, "Son, never grow old". While I was still in the robust bloom of life, this prophetic statement fell upon not deaf but certainly immature ears. Aging or at least the feeling of the effects of aging was still some years off. It is only lately that I fully appreciate her lament. Growing old is a pain in the . . . well: fingers, back, knees, occasionally the arms, neck and, with the inclusion of hemorrhoids, the anal sphincter to finish the phrase.

For those who are still too immature to empathize with this statement, aging is a strange process. The body slows down, shifts shape, sags, aches, does all manner of things you only heard old people complain of. All the while, the mind remains the mind of a twenty-five year old. For the male, it manifests itself when some winsome bimbo slinks by in a tea shirt and jeans some three sizes too small. You know you're aging when you pull in your gut and it remains perched precariously on the belt buckle. Recently, I passed a couple of blooming bimbos, went through my instinctive male ego adjustment and saw a reflection of a bald, grey-haired, fat old man in the store window behind. Who was that old fart? My heavens, it was me! The paradox of the real and the imagined came crashing down upon my psyche. To quote the wise sage: never grow old.

Another effect of aging is the seeming fleeting of time. To a young person, the passage of a month seems forever. To one my age, last year was just yesterday. As I survey my shrinking, aging domain now, I notice that my present pussycat: Bob is aging also. Bob came to us as a young adult, and according to my spouse, we've had him (or he, us) for some twelve years. Come to think of it, he has been looking a little seedy of late. His sides seem to droop and his face looks a little thinner. Gad zooks, Bob is an old fart too!

I have noticed that he has become much more a creature of habit. He had many bad habits to start with. At least they are now predictable. As old people have the reputation of becoming crotchety, Bob, who was crotchety as a youth, has become even more so. Now when I interrupt his early morning, mid-morning, early afternoon, afternoon or late afternoon snooze, he growls his displeasure in a most threatening falsetto sound. He's become downright grumpy.

The morning begins by letting Bob emerge from his nighttime sanctuary in the basement and eating his breakfast. After his meal, I let, or rather encourage, him outside. I've been doing it for years. He knows the routine as well as I. Of late, he doesn't take kindly to going outside, especially when the temperature is below freezing or it is raining or snowing. True, I don't think much of going out in less than perfect conditions either, but I have no control on the weather. Now he goes through a hissing and grunting routine that I suppose is to frighten me. He knows that I would give him a good kick in the butt if he ever acted upity with me, so it is a shallow threat. I attribute it to his advanced age . . . which is on a par with me, for good or ill.

I've also noticed that Bob has become quite talkative in a catly sort of way. Not only does he meow for food or attention as in the past, but lately he looks you in the eye and just talks. It's not a meow in the strictest sense, but it is a cat communication. He's saying something, and is quite content if you respond in kind. Whenever we close a door for privacy, Bob lets us know of his indignation. The tone is definitely one of displeasure. He feels that there should be no secrets in the household. Perhaps pussycats can contract paranoia.

Sometimes he just walks into the room and talks for the sake of talking. Perhaps he just needs the reassurance that his support system is still intact. He talks and we talk for some time just exchanging mutually unintelligible sounds; but it seems to have a calming effect. Calm is a term that has eluded his persona until quite recently.

Bob has also become quite lovable. By this I mean he seeks out affection to a greater degree than in the past. Lately, when we are sitting down, he has taken to climbing on us, putting his paws on our shoulders and draping his torso over our chests, shoving his face into our neck and purring loudly. As one ages and comes to the realization that independent existence gets more difficult with each passing day, it is nice to know that you still have friends.

Bob is the only cat I have ever had grow old. Having always lived in a rural environment, my pussycats have all gone the way of country cats. Life in the raw rural world is not gentle. To survive in the country requires more than nine lives. The suburban lifestyle, however, is conducive to a long and happy life if one can avoid automobile traffic.

There is little to disturb feline domestic bliss other than an occasional scrap with an overly invasive neighbor. The latter always seems to occur at two in the morning much to my chagrin. Cat disputes are usually more noise than combat. My human neighbors have indulged my extended family's nocturnal disruptions of their sleep by never mentioning the episodes. I know they are just being tolerant. One would have to be totally deaf not to be awakened by the uproar.

Bob has always been the feline scourge of the neighborhood. His exploits as the neighborhood bully have become legendary. All manner of dogs and cats of any size or sex have bowed deference or suffered the consequences for many years now. But all things must come to an end. Age catches up with even the most feared gunslinger, imaginative ladies man or precocious pussycat. Age has made Bob a victim of his past. Several of the formerly cowed youthful tom cats have now grown to maturity, and have harbored a natural vengeance on the aging bully.

Two rather large toms now seem to take great delight in strutting across Bob's shrinking domain. A big, seedy looking grey guy is the most imposing. He looks like a true campaigner. When Bob sees him approaching, he hot foots it into the house and screams his displeasure in a tirade of hisses, growls, and grunts through the safety of the plate glass slider. Both toms strut brazenly by just to annoy Bob; topping off their bluster with a good squirt on my shrubs just for added insult.

We first noticed this transition from precocious pest to passive pussy just this last year. We became aware of this change one morning when a sound like a cross between a fire truck siren and fingernails along a chalkboard interrupted the family breakfast. Upon searching for the strange sound, we found Bob in a most agitated condition watching a challenger despoil his turf. It was such an unusual cacophony of sounds that we just laughed ourselves into childlike joviality.

Bob even punctuated the siren call with spits and hisses that looked and sounded quite ferocious. I sure as heck didn't want to put my hand near by. One does not try to fondle or pet a pussy in the middle of a feline dispute. But I later discovered that it was all aural bravado.

In the past, we would let Bob out to exercise his property rights. This time, when we opened the slider for him, he seemed to be in a quandary. Bob gave us a look of one betrayed. "Et tu Brute and your laughing wife." With terror in his eyes, he took off toward the living room for cover. Bob didn't want any part of his haughty nemesis. This was the first time he had ever lost face. My guess is that he had lost not only his face, but a good bit of his fur and hide at some earlier encounter. It was then that we realized that Bob was aging. He wasn't the man, or pussycat, he used to be. At least he had the good sense to recognize it. I haven't quite come to grips with my reality yet. I still give the "bird" to youthful reckless drivers.

The periodic confrontational caterwauling has become not only routine, but frequent. While it engenders a great deal of human laughter, it remains quite innocuous. One of Bob's nemeses has even got the gall to come face to face against the window. This really infuriates Bob. The tom's insulting squirt in Bob's face on the glass now infuriates me. Bob and I have both become grumpy old men.

This has caused Bob to become quite nervous in his old age. As Bob sits in the sun behind the glass slider, I have only to say in a challenging way, "Where is he, Bob. Watch him!" and poor Bob goes into his hissing and growling routine. I have conditioned poor Bob like Pavlov's dog. The entertainment value of the situation complete with sound and fury is just too much for my devilish nature. I'm afraid I tease the poor old fart. But then, my wife and the neighborhood youngsters tease me about my aging bald head.

Perhaps it is the plight of the old to reap what they have sown in their youth. To paraphrase an old Amish saying: "We grow too soon old and too late smart." I should have listened to my wise old mother and never grown old. But then, do we have a choice?

The Tenth Life

Each morning in my retirement, I get together with a bunch of old geezers like myself and have coffee down at the old country store. While I'm not the oldest, I have to admit that I'm not the youngest. But to give my reader an incite into our ages, the couple of single guys in the group go to the local nursing home to pick up girls. Like Archie Bunker, we remember Glen Miller, the Hit Parade, and LaSalles. We sit around, drink coffee, solve the world's greatest problems, and of course, shoot the bull. With the longevity of eighty plus years multiplied by some ten old coots, the array of stories retrieved from the collective memory is quite entertaining. Needless to say, humorous incidents from the past are not only interesting, they reinforce the cliché that the truth is stranger than fiction. In that we live in a rural environment, stories of past animal acquaintances are prevalent. Cats and dogs and all manner of beasties have contributed to the collective psyche. Incredible tales of journeys and narrow escapes of pet critters are common place. After a few tales, one begins to believe that the lower animals aren't really very low on the old intelligence scale. One of my fellow geezers related a story about a pet cat he had as a youth back in New Jersey.

It seems that for years, the family cat lived a normal, uncomplicated life; using up his nine lives in a most mundane existence. But as happens to all God's creatures, we grow old an infirmed. One day a sizeable growth on the cat's side became evident. The local veterinarian pronounced the imminent demise of the poor tabby. For the astronomical fee of twenty-five dollars, the vet would "put him down." But this story was back when a good used Chevrolet could be purchased for two hundred dollars. My first car as a teenager was twenty-nine dollars; and that was from a car dealer. My friend's father declined the vet's offer and reluctantly decided to do the deed himself.

As a hunter, his dad felt he could do it humanely with his shotgun. All that was required was to take the poor tabby out in the country, give it a bowl of his favorite food; and while he was enjoying his final meal, dad would shoot him. Hopefully, the blast would be quick and painless. For twenty-five dollars, dad could endure the mental anguish! His young son would have to go along to aid in the ill-famed event.

When the day of infamy arrived, the cat, shotgun, can of cat food, favorite dish, dad and son took a ride out in the country. A secluded spot was found and the stage was set for the coup d' grace. Euthanasia always requires a euphemism. Tabby, so called because I don't believe the poor cat's name was ever mentioned in the tale, was given his favorite food in his favorite dish. My friend's dad backed off several paces and prepared. Ready! Aim! Kabloom!

Just as Tabby was about to partake of his food, the dish suddenly vanished before his nose. He looked rather puzzled. Where did the darn thing go? The dish no doubt became an array of garbage splattered chards over in the next county, but the cat stood there unharmed and puzzled at the disappearance of his food dish. My friend's dad, equally puzzled at the unexpected change of events, made the statement: "That cat was surely not meant to die like that!"

My friend, his dad, Tabby and the shotgun returned to his home where, the story continued, Tabby's tumor shrank back to normalcy and Tabby lived for another couple of years. Tabby surely had a tenth life to live.

Finale

Even in the world of Morris, Garfield and Heathcliff, a common pussycat leads a precarious existence. By law, they enjoy only the status of human chattel. Without the protection of a human, they have no rights or privileges beyond what the worst in our human society wishes to accord. A vagabond tom, for instance, doesn't even rate the protection that rabbits and groundhogs enjoy. At least they have an agency of government that enforces a reasonable status under the game laws. Even the lowly fish have legal status under numerous laws. Pussycats are nonentities. Only crazy cat people or we who just like cats for their own sake are their sole hope for their future on this overcrowded planet.

As a youngster, I was influenced by the many cat haters who convinced me that cats really were evil creatures. They are sneaky, vicious killers. Later, as a neophyte hunter, I was again influenced by the "old timers" that pussycats killed game. Why if it wasn't for cats, the fields and woods would be teaming with small game animals. I'm sure I passed this "truth" along to some other youthful mind. I hope that it didn't cause the unnecessary demise of some poor innocent household pussycat. With the exception of a pussycat that was a family member before I was old enough to know, we were primarily a dog family, so I had no point of reference other than the parade of hobos that frequented our neighborhood. They seemed to be O.K.

I liked all animals, but I had learned to be a cat bigot. I didn't go out of my way to do them harm, but then, I didn't go out of my way to be friendly. They did. They would rub up against me as if we were old buddies. I would ignore their gestures of friendship just because it is easier to be a closed minded bigot than a confused open minded thinker. When you are the ripe old age of six, you are apt to allow adults to do your thinking for you.

As I stated, when I was very, very young, we had a cat. I should say my mother had a cat. We were living in an apartment I barely remember, upstairs over a friend of my mother's who could tell when the cat was running along the floor. It made a noise like the rabbit that had a bit part in the movie: Bambi. The rabbit, hence the cat, were named Thumper. My mother was a cat lover. In later times, I accused her of becoming a full fledged cat person which she didn't deny. What I recall of Thumper was only a traumatic experience; one of those experiences that flesh is ere to while growing up in the inner city.

The inner city is not one city but a collection of "blocks". These blocks mark the boundary lines of the "turf" of the youth. They demark the ends of the known world for inner city youths aged two to eighteen, beyond which reside the uncivilized aliens who comprise the rest of us. I'm convinced that these arbitrary boundaries are identical to the tribal boundaries of natives all over the world. If they were to draw maps and exchange ambassadors, they would be exactly like the world boundaries that we take for granted in our "civilized" and sophisticated world. Like the latter, there is a group identity, a social cohesion, a set of well understood but not necessarily written laws, and they are patrolled by the area's young warriors.

An unwarranted intrusion into the recognized boundaries by an alien individual or group is met by swift, determined, and blind aggression. The only exceptions were corridors that allowed passage to and from the various stores that supplied the bodily needs of the inhabitants. Deviate from the straight and narrow path and one might wear a scar or a crooked nose for life. Some of the more valiant actually cherished their mutilation as a mark of courage.

This code of territorial integrity is extended to any dogs or cats that belong to the alien group as well. Dogs have the good survival sense to "turn tail" and retreat. They may not understand the laws of human inconsistency, but they are smart enough to know when to retreat to more familiar turf. Cats, on the other hand, are not so much disposed to understand the queer behavior of humans. They are more likely to cower and remain stationary to defend their little fannies. This makes them frequent casualties in the territorial drives of the human animal. Thumper was such a casualty.

The next block was known to the youths of our block as the Dumbarton gang. It was a rare occasion that they would venture into our block or vice versa. But within their block, they were the undisputed rulers and arch villains of our 41st Street gang. Thumper, by residence, was also a member whether she wished it or not. An extensive spy network identified gang cats and dogs from the transient hobos that passed usually unmolested through the inner ćity maize.

Thumper disappeared one day. I was too young to understand the significance. Some days later, one of the neighborhood youths discovered the grisly remains of Thumper. With youthful curiosity and excitement, I went to look at the remains of our pussycat. The Dumbarton gang, or at least it was assumed, had caught Thumper on the fringe of their turf. Thumper had been wired to a stake and burned Joan of Arc fashion in the high wooden fenced back yard of a small hardware store. It was the first experience that I remember of the fallibility of life and the possibility of a violent death; a little but not important bit of history; except to me and mine.

Hunters, like youthful gang members, seem to have irrational and misplaced hatred. This hatred is directed against cats. If a pussycat is caught roaming the hills at the same time some hunter passes by, the cat is, more often than not, doomed. This occurs even when the cat is legally on his owner's land and the hunter is trespassing. Might makes right in the case of cats. Gladys, our little unfit mother who never grew up, came home one day dragging her insides. She had two bullet holes through her. Even with what care I could immediately offer, she died before we could even get ready to leave for the vet. How she managed to survive as long as she did was a wonder. It seemed that she just wanted to come home and die among friends.

Ajax, the poor handicapped pussycat that dragged his lifeless tail for the last two years of his life, disappeared on the opening day of hunting season. In that he was pure white, there was no way he could be mistaken for game. He was just in the wrong spot at the wrong time.

If statistics were compiled on the manner of death of pussycats, I believe violent death would be most common. Of the many cats that I have had or have had me, only one died in bed; or in her box as the case may be. Of the many, only Samantha, my fat little sister, died naturally. I assume she died of a heart attack brought on by exertion. One day, Sam didn't show up for chow. For Sam to miss food was an ominous sign. Food was Sam's sine qua non.

As with the many other cats, we feared foul play. We were living in the country at the time. Sam was not the only cat with us. It wasn't until the evening that my wife found Sam. She was curled into her box on top of a gardening table that was on the back porch. It appeared that she died in her sleep. She looked at peace. Out of family respect, I placed Sam in a blue velvet bag along with two cans of her favorite cat food and buried her under the apple tree that graced the view in the front of the house.

All of the other cats that formed a part of my life died violent deaths. Amos, the little fish eater, was killed by a car. A college student trying to shave twelve seconds from the time it takes to get nowhere in particular ran over Amos. Amos crawled to the gutter and died. The student never even slowed down. Cats' lives are not that important in human affairs.

As a teenager, I traveled with other teenagers who took great delight in trying to squash cats that managed to venture on to the roads. One in particular painted little cat silhouettes on his fender in the manner of World War II aviators. As I recall, he had quite a few "kills". I personally have run over three cats in my lifetime. All three were in my youth, all three were under identical circumstances, and none was intentional.

The first was at the age of twelve. I was riding my bicycle down a country road when suddenly, a cat darted out of the bushes right under my front wheel. Needless to say, he caused more damage to me than I caused to him. He squealed and continued running. I lost my balance and came crashing down to a skin scraping stop. At that precise moment I was in no mood to feel either concern or remorse at the plight of my partner in pain. To this day, I believe I am the only human to have run over a cat with a bicycle.

The second was two years later. As youth gives way to maturity, I had graduated to a Cushman motor scooter. In nearly identical fashion, a cat ran under the front wheel of the scooter. Fortunately for me, the greater weight of the scooter allowed me to keep upright. Unfortunately for the cat, I'm sure the greater weight hurt. I'm equally sure that it wasn't a lethal injury. My adolescent frame plus the weight of the scooter didn't equal the weight of my present overweight carcass. In that my poor Bob cat has survived my accidental big footed squashings, I'm sure the unfortunate pussycat survived my scooter and me.

The third was several years later. I was now a full grown adult. I even had a full grown adult toy; a vintage automobile. Again, along a similar country road edged with similar bushes, a cat ran out in front of me. I heard the sickening thump as the tire went over him. As before, he squealed and ran off. I tried to find him but couldn't. I'm sure he was hurting; and most likely died. I did feel remorse. What I can't understand is how some people don't. I remember every creature that I have killed in this manner: one dog, three rabbits, a squirrel, three snakes, a robin, a meadow lark and a pheasant. For some reason, my remorse doesn't extend to the snakes; and the pheasant was promptly eaten for dinner.

I wouldn't be surprised if my present little bugger, Bob, didn't meet with a violent end. He has no fear of dogs, people, or other cats. In his communion with men, he has been known to lie out in the middle of the street and watch the cars drive around him. In that the circle is sometimes used by drivers who are seeking even faster routes to get somewhere, some day he will just be in the way. Not that there is anything of importance in this community for which to get there any sooner, it is just that people are in a hurry to arrive there for the sake of arriving.

If it isn't a car, it will be a cat hater. There is one in the community who has a reputation of bragging about the number of cats he has dispatched with his rifle. With the state of justice heavily weighted in favor of the unsavory, a pussycat doesn't stand much of a chance. Fortunately, Bob doesn't wander that far, but who knows what the future will offer?

Dogs are potential killers of pussycats. When I was still a youth, we had a dog in the neighborhood named "Nosey". Nosey was a mongrel, the greater part of which was Malamute. Nosey was big. For some reason, Nosey was endowed by nature to be the epitome of the dog versus cat conflict. Nosey could kill a cat with two shakes of the head. She was a master of feline execution. I've never seen another dog quite as skilled as Nosey, although I have seen some pretty efficient cat killers. I've seen some tom cats put up a good fight and even put much larger dogs to flight, but I have never seen a cat kill a dog. In this conflict, the cat is the proverbial underdog or undercat as the case might be.

I have run across innumerable dead cats in my life. All had met violent deaths. One stranger died in my garage. She had a bullet hole in her, and somehow found respite in my garage. Another, or rather several pieces of another, were found under my house in Tennessee. I'm sure, judging by the patches of fur that survived the dismemberment, it was a transient tom from the next farm. He must have come a'courting at my place. I had several eligible young ladies at the time, but a country tom must get permission from the army of resident dog brothers before he takes liberties on someone else's turf.

Some day, I hope that I will have a very old cat. I have seen a few, but very few. Cats live in a world of live fast, die young, and leave good memories and lots of kittens. The precarious place of American catdom seems to insure that few pussycats will collect any form of social security. For all their trouble and heart ache, I do love pussycats. I like them for themselves. As fellow beings, they have taught me much about themselves, about myself, about human nature, and about life in general. While there are thousands of books about cats, life, and truth, few people have the time to read them. Where a picture is worth a thousand words, a cat is worth a thousand books. If one wishes to know life, read a book. If one wishes to live life, get a cat. They'll fill your life just as fully as they have mine. I wouldn't have missed them for the world.

The End

From *Thoughts of an Aging Mind* —

Cats

Arrogant apostates living astride two worlds
At once both nature's savage predator child
And hedonistic domestic pampered progeny
Safely concealing their relentless call of the wild

Most resourceful of all man's animal adherents
Clever sycophants flattering their pretend god
With charm and grace extracting their lord's
    bounty
Enthralling humans with furtive glance or nod

Captivating supposed masters with their charms
Like worldly-wise courtesans of a royal court
Their devious wild natures hidden by their beauty
Controlling their humans as if it were a sport

Beguiling naive man to youthful adoration
With supple muscular limbs and winsome displays
Exotic enthralling eyes holding secrets deep
    within
Connoting to man their brutish instinctual ways

Is there a man that could not but love a kitten?
They can melt the coldest and hardest of closed
    hearts
The unspoiled and virginal qualities of carefree
    youth
Still ignorant and free of the lethal and cunning
    arts

163

Yet in their boisterous and seeming frantic play
Lay the seeds of all murderous predatory
    strategies
Now performed on innocent dust-bunnies stirred
    by wind
On hapless victims later perfecting their honed
    abilities

The mature cat in both form and function
    beautiful
Their colors and textures in near infinite perfect
    design
Their movements a rhythmic symphony of bone
    and sinew
Their bearing and graceful composure looks
    almost divine

What exuded pleasure is gleaned from the act of
    purring?
Perplexed man is destined to never know
The apparent ecstasy of prolonged seeming
    mental euphoria
Is there a psychic place of which mankind can
    never go?

This nation's most desirable pet of choice
From poor man's backwoods cabin to rich estate
Cats charm and entertain their credulous human
    mentors
And enjoy a most desirable even enviable fate

Cat's Eyes

What mystery in a cat's eye lies therein?
That deeply buried hint of a deadly urge
Held rampant through all of their predatory kin
Where both lover and killer's telling glances
    merge

By day a look of strange yet comely wonder
By night a piercing spark of reflective fire
Always the furtive look of the charming beguiler
A guise that mankind has come to greatly admire

The eerie slit of black in crystal green amber
A mysterious look of murderous far away thought
The dispassionate gaze of the deadly poisonous
    adder
A unique paradigm of what Mother Nature has
    wrought

I sit and watch my playful cute little kitten
And witness the cunning moves and vigilant stare
From playful pet to potential killer in transition
No hint of which to read in its feline glare

It is written that eyes are windows of the soul
Can this be true for even our feline friends?
Eyes with primal predatory savagery extol
Yet with pampered domesticity contends

165